THE VATICAN

Edited by Francesco Papafava

SCALA

CONTENTS

Introduction, 3

St. Peter's, *by Laura Draghi*, 4

The Vatican Gardens, *by Francesco Papafava*, 41

The Papal Palace and the Vatican Museums, *by Lucia Cecchi*, 50

Index of Popes and Artists, 96

© Copyright 1984 by SCALA, Istituto Fotografico Editoriale, Firenze
Editing: Ezra Nahmad
Layout: Francesco Forte
Translation: Carol Wasserman
Produced by SCALA
Photographs: SCALA (A. Corsini, M. Falsini, N. Grifoni, F. Papafava, M. Sarri), except: inside front cover and nos. 4, 55 (Pubbliaerfoto); nos. 12, 14, 16 and p. 24 no. II (Fabbrica di S. Pietro); nos. 11, 20, 54 (Toni Niccolini); no. 33 (Bruno del Priore); p. 25 nos. III, VI (Attualità Fotografica Giordani); p. 24 no. I, p. 54 no. II (Felici); p. 19 nos. III, IV and p. 25 no. IV (Santoni Lido); title page (Biblioteca Vaticana); nos. 92, 93, 94, 95, 96, 97, 98, 99, 100, 101, 102, 103, 104, 105, 106, 107, 108, 109 (Musei Vaticani)
Type-set by A-Z, Florence
Printed in Italy by KINA Italia, Milan - 1994

Cover photo: The Dome of St. Peter's.

Inside front cover: Aerial view of the basilica and St. Peter's Square.

Inside back cover: Plan of the Vatican City.

Back cover: Inside the Sistine Chapel.

Title page: Coats of arms of John Paul II (left) and the Vatican City (right).

p. 96: Medallion showing Bernini's plans for St. Peter's (Vatican Library).

1. *Via della Conciliazione; in the distance, the façade of St. Peter's.*

The unmistakable dome of St. Peter's catches and cata-lyzes the attention of first-time visitors to Rome. But even without the guide that this image and symbol of the Vatican affords, pilgrims and visitors know what to look for within the Vatican walls. Although the city only recently became a sovereign state, its history dates back to antiquity.

For almost two thousand years pilgrims have come to the Vatican from all corners of the world to venerate the memory of the apostle Peter, to pray at the tombs of more recent pontiffs, to hear the pope speak, and to watch the sacred celebrations in St. Peter's.

The Vatican is traditionally the spiritual center of Christianity, and provides tangible evidence of its roots. With the passage of time it has become a mirror of Medi-terranean artistic culture, too, beginning in the fifteenth century when the papacy became an interpreter of the clas-sical inheritance of Rome and promotor of Renaissance culture. As a result of the immense efforts that the popes dedicated to archaeology and museum building in the eighteenth and nineteenth centuries, the Vatican offers one of the more complete and modern examples of museum activi-ty in the world today.

This book is intended as an introduction to these two aspects—the religious and the artistic—and to the nume-rous other stimuli that the visitor to the Vatican may re-ceive. The editor has thought it suitable to back up the two major chapters on St. Peter's and the Vatican Museums with a few shorter chapters which briefly illustrate the his-toric development and the present organization of the State of Vatican City. The latter was officially established in 1929, but il was already alluded to in the aftermath of the occupation of Rome, by a farsighted law promulgated unilaterally by Italy's new government (Legge delle Guar-entigie, 13 May 1871) which granted the Catholic Church the freedom to carry out its spiritual activity un-disturbed. Cardinal Giovanni Battista Montini, the fu-ture Pope Paul VI, in a reference to the end of the Papal States, was to praise that activity with the following words:

"Providence—now we see it clearly—had ar-ranged things differently... the pope went away... humiliated by the loss of temporal power even in his own city, Rome. But as is known, he then resumed with uncommon vigor his role as master of life and witness of the Gospel, and achieved more in the spiritul government of the church and in the moral leadership of the world than ever before" (from L'Osservatore Romano, 12 October 1962).

2

3

2. Statue of St. Peter (Giuseppe de Fabris, 1838), on the left side of the steps.

3. Statue of St. Paul (Adamo Tadolini, 1838); companion piece of the statue of St. Peter, on the right side of the steps.

4. Aerial view of the Vatican city, on the right bank of the Tiber; in the foreground, Ponte Sant'Angelo and Hadrian's Mausoleum (Castel Sant'Angelo).

5. St. Peter's Square, viewed from the terrace on the basilica roof; on the left and right is Bernini's colonnade, in the center the Egyptian Obelisk.

SAINT PETER'S
by Laura Draghi

Meeting St. Peter's

The pilgrim or visitor to the Vatican who desires a gradual, aesthetically and emotionally correct approach to the whole meaning of St. Peter's must begin at the Ponte Sant'Angelo on the Tiber and walk up the grand boulevard called Via della Conciliazione, with its human bustle and heavy traffic.

This wide, straight boulevard adorned by a procession of obelisk-shaped streetlamps, a feat of triumphalism styled on the spirit of its makers—it was built in 1933—was more than just criticized: its very right to exist was questioned because it called for the demolition of the history-laden medieval quarter and left the basilica façade exposed and seemingly deprived of its mystery. Nevertheless, to do the case justice, one must bear in mind that the roadway designed by the architects Marcello Piacentini and Attilio Spaccarelli resolved a serious, age old traffic problem and completed the final phase of a complex program initiated during the Renaissance by Bramante. The program was taken up by Carlo Fontana, who recommended the demolition of the "island" constituted by the medieval Borgo. It later reappeared in several resolutions of the *Reverenda Fabbrica di San Pietro* (St. Peter's building works) and in a "notice" published during the papacy of Innocent X, who looked forward to the construction of a great axial roadway to "give greater majesty to the temple of St. Peter and greater beauty to the Vatican City." Thus, if in the past the sudden, unexpected appearance of St. Peter's just outside the body of the Borgo caused immense surprise, today the solemn, generous promise announced from afar by the basilica, the dome, and the square must impress with equally intense emotion the visitor who advances toward Gian Lorenzo Bernini's great colonnade, "the embrace of St. Peter to the world".

This "colonnaded theater," as it was called in a document of 1657, is one of the greatest achievements of urban architecture. It was the exclusive idea of "Cavalier Bernino," who obtained the commission from Pope Alexander VII Chigi in 1656 and completed the work in eleven years. The grandiose aspect of the complex derives partly from its dimensions—a maximum width of 244 meters, and a 340-meter run from the granite strip of the Vatican border (where Bernini wanted to place another colonnade) to the foot of the stairway. But it also derives from the proportioned volumes of columns, façade and dome, and from the illusionistic effects of an incomparable scenography. We are all acquainted with the most spectacular of these effects. Anyone standing on one of the two marble disks which mark off the two foci of the elliptical piazza will find to his astonishment that the columns of the three outer rows of curves have disappeared behind the columns of the inner curve. Bernini obtained this effect by gradually increasing the column diameters from the inner to the outer rows so that the distance between them was kept always constant. The travertine columns are 16 meters high and number 246. The largest ones have a diameter of 142 centimeters. There are 88 pilasters and 140 statues of the saints atop the entablature. The

4

5

6

7

states, produced in Bernini's workshop, are over 3 meters high and create a beautiful choral effect.

The absolute protagonist of the square is the basilica. But its arcane, bold interlocutor is the red granite Egyptian obelisk that originally stood beside St. Peter's. It was removed to its present position in 1586, a feat immediately inscribed in the legendary epic of Italian engineering. The over 25-meter-high monolith dates back to 1935 B.C. and is mentioned by Pliny in his *Natural History*. It was imported by the Emperor Caligula for his Circus Vaticanus, later called the Circus of Nero, where Peter was martyred, to be buried in the vicinity afterwards by his small, persecuted flock of Christians. The obelisk thus represents more than just the prestigious embellishment of the square that grew up around it a century after its relocation there. It is one of the antecedents of the cult of St. Peter and the very first milestone in its history, a colossal "relic by contact," in no way different from the more modest relics that are worshipped by Christians for having touched the bodies of the saints. There was a legend—even Boccaccio liked it—which claimed that at the very top of the great "needle" an urn with Julius Caesar's ashes lay. But today the bronze cross of the cusp holds a fragment of the "true cross," a symbolic reminder of the mystical bond between the cross of the Redeemer and the upside-down cross—reversed, it is said, as a profession of unworthiness—of his first follower and successor.

The two great, elegant fountains with three superimposed ba-

8

9

6. Colonnade of St. Peter's Square (Gian Lorenzo Bernini, 1656-66), left wing; statues of saints by Bernini's followers stand atop the trabeation.

7. Three-basin fountain by Carlo Maderno (1613), on the right side of the square.

8. Bernini's fountain, added in 1675 as a companion piece of Maderno's.

9. St. Peter's Square; behind the colonnade is the papal palace; on the right, the building erected by Sixtus V, with the present apartment of the pope.

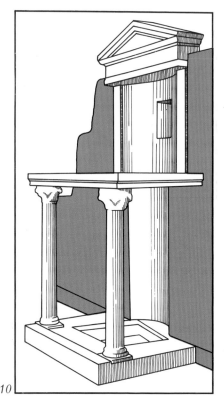

10

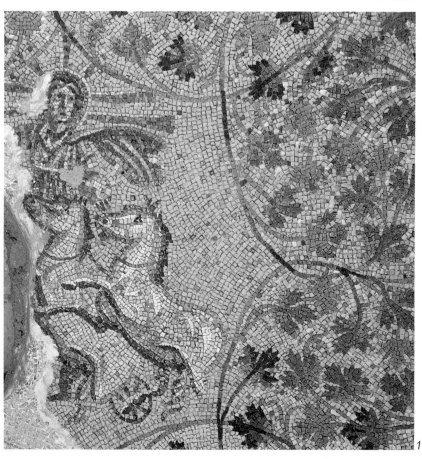

11

10. *Reconstruction of the so-called Trophy of Gaius; the shrine of the apostle, Peter, was erected around A.D. 150 against the "red wall."*

11. *Vatican Necropolis, mosaic in mausoleum M with Christ-Helios, symbol of the Resurrection (A.D. 100-150).*

sins, positioned by Maderno and Bernini, sweeten and refresh the magnificent, desert-like expanse of the square with their abundant play of water, and soften the solitary severity of the obelisk aligned with the fountains along the main axis.

St. Peter's Square, a closed yet infinitely vast stretch of space, a sacred enclosure open to the visit of the multitudes, is the theater of the day-to-day history of the Catholic Church so closely entwined with universal history. Here is the highly evocative point of arrival and departure—the "at last I am here, but not yet there"—for the visitor who has left the world behind.

Return to the Roots: A Pagan Necropolis and Christian Cemetery.

To truly understand St. Peter's, the visitor must take a step back from the basilica, both in spirit and in deed, and begin his pilgrimage at the root that nourished the visible heart of Christianity and made it grow through the centuries, namely, the *martyrium* of the Apostle Peter, one of the many tombs of the pagan-Christian necropolis partially brought to light during the pontificate of Pius XII.

Visits to the necropolis must be planned in advance, for a permit (obtained by mail from the Reverenda Fabbrica di S. Pietro, 00120 Città del Vaticano), must be shown at the entrance. From here one passes through the *Arco delle Campane*, the Arch of the Bells (the oldest bell of all, the *Campana della Predica*, dates from 1288) beneath the watchful eyes of the Swiss Guards, crosses the Piazza dei Proto-

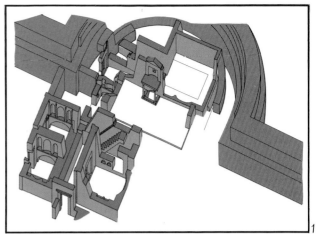

12

13

14

martiri, walks along the dusty outer wall constructed by Michel-angelo, and descends into the dusky chambers of the Vatican Grottoes amongst archaeological exhibits from the basilica of Con-stantine, to a world without time. Here is the first- to fourth-century burial place that grew up along the road that bordered the Circus of Nero. It was used by pagans and Christians alike, but with one difference: the pagans called it a *necròpolis*, a "city of the dead," the Christians a *coemeterium*, a "land of sleeping men." Sleep meant life, and the Christians lived on in Christ after death.

Although it was not quite a city, the burial ground was surely a long, long, open-air village which reached as far as the Tiber to the east. Along both sides of the underground path in use today are rows of mausoleums or family chapels decorated with paintings and mosaics, and containing loculi for the ashes of the cremated and sar-cophagi or earthen tombs for the bodies of the inhumed, the latter unquestionably including the Christians. The people of this land of the dead were a heterogeneous lot—mainly wealthy, extending over thirteen or fourteen generations and professing an infinite variety of philosophies and creeds.

This necropolis-cemetery was destroyed by an unprecedented act of violence in the fourth century A.D. When a military victory and the advice of his pious mother, St. Helen, converted Constantine to Christianity, he blotted out the ancient burial ground beneath an avalanche of rubble and earth in what appears to be a perfect exam-ple of "architectural folly" on the part of an imperial builder (who is hardly to be suspected of professional incompetence!). Constantine undertook to level *Mons Vaticanus*, the Vatican Hill, in order to erect

12. The extant lane of the Vatican Necro-polis; in the right-hand wall are the mauso-leums.

13. Reconstruction of Camp P and of Con-stantine's apse, in the Necropolis.

14. Section plan of St. Peter's with the Sa-cred Grottoes and the Necropolis beneath the floor of the present building.

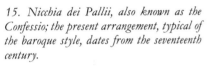

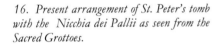

15

16

15. *Nicchia dei Pallii, also known as the Confessio; the present arrangement, typical of the baroque style, dates from the seventeenth century.*

16. *Present arrangement of St. Peter's tomb with the Nicchia dei Pallii as seen from the Sacred Grottoes.*

the Basilica of St. Peter's in a most illogical place. There can be only one explanation for this act of sacrilege (to put it mildly) and for the costs and difficulties of so technically bold and complex a project, and it lies in the absolute necessity of placing the future altar of the pope upon a certain tomb, which for over a century and a half had been a highly important cult object. Even the walls speak of its importance—literally, not figuratively. Near the end of the open part of the cemetery, the chapels and tombs suddenly crowd together like so many members of a bold but respectful assembly closing in around an exceptional person or thing. The Christian symbols on the walls—the shepherd, the fisherman, the anchor, the vine, Jonah and the whale, and the radiant chariot of the sun identified with Christos-Helios—increase in number. But the structures and symbols end at a certain point and at that point an empty space begins. The archaeologists call it "Camp P." It's background is a red brick wall and it is empty, clearly, because it is sacred: because, according to tradition, at the foot of this wall, close to the site of his martyrdom, the apostle Peter was buried. And tradition is supported by the nonsense of Constantine's urbanistic projects and confirmed by the findings of archaeology. To the right of Camp P is a low wall completely covered with graffiti scribbled by unknown authors. They may have been uneducated fanatics or even worse, but here they are the benefactors of human history, for their scribblings are documentary "sources" of inestimable value. The graffiti are brief prayers to Christ and Peter. They consist in the Constantinian cross with the motto "in him you will triumph" and, more important, the laconic *Petros eni* (Peter is here) iscribed in the loculus in which in 1953 the archaeologist Margherita Guarducci found some very unusual bones and fragments. Her discovery led to some major conclusions. Firstly, it is now held that even if the remains are not those of Peter, the loculus is surely his tomb; secondly, that in pre-Constantinian times an aedicula or small altar was backed up against the "red wall"; and thirdly, that the bones buried on the latter site were transferred by Constantine to the safer, dryer loculus of Wall g ("g" for graffiti) and later sealed in the "memoria"—the Constantinian altar at the base of the

17. *Chapel of St. Peter, Sacred Grottoes; visible beyond the grille on the altar is the marble of the marble of the early Constantinian monument; the decorative program dates from the pontificate of Clement VII (late sixteenth century).*

18. *Statue of St. Peter Enthroned, Sacred Grottoes; the torso comes from a third century B.C. statue of a philosopher, the head and hands date from the fifteenth century.*

17

later altars built by Pope Gregory the Great (590-604), Pope Callixtus II (1119-24), and Pope Clement VII (1592-1605). Today, after braving a complex maze of passageways, one may rest one's eyes on this "root" of St. Peter's in the loculus of Wall g. There, behind a sheet of glass, in a modest, irregular niche are the meagre remains of the man upon whom this great basilica was founded.

The Vatican Grottoes

The area between the ancient necropolis and the floor of the present church still contains parts of the Constantinian basilica and the semicircular crypt that pope Gregory the Great built by raising the presbytery around 600 A.D. The surrounding ambulatory and the three low aisles are sixteenth-century additions. The twentieth century saw to the functional and aesthetic restoration of the New Grottoes—the area now open to visitors. And the most recent work of all is the architectural rehabilitation of the wall that separated the nave and the crypt and that now provides a view, through a small, glassed-in arch, of the "Confessio"—the splendid seventeenth-century monument for St. Peter's tomb with the Niche of the Pallia, where the sacred stoles of the newly-elected metropolitan bishops are kept. The modern "window" undoubtedly robs this holy place of part of its mystery, but the bold gesture of the Gothic angels on each

The Constantinian Basilica
by Francesco Papafava

A modest tomb, a small commemorative monument and a great basilica built to exalt the saint's burial place and receive the devotion of pilgrims from every part of the earth: this, in a word, is the meaning of St. Peter's.

The first surviving mention of the tomb of St. Peter comes from Gaius the presbyter, an authoritative Roman clergyman who lived between the second and the third centuries A.D.

To prove the supremacy of the Church of Rome over the Eastern Churches, Gaius's writing thundered out that it was the Vatican to hold the "trophy" of the founder, St. Peter, Vicar of Christ.

The trophy was a monument commemorating a victory—in the case of the Christians, the victory of faith over death. The trophy mentioned by Gaius was a modest aedicula tomb composed of two superimposed niches divided by a travertine slab resting on two colonettes. According to indisputable archaeological findings, the small "memoria"—1.80 m. long and 2.30 m. high—was built sometime in the 260s A.D.

apse, set in a rectangular, marble-coated prism—the Constantinian monument—visible from the nave through a double door. From the lower niche, which more or less corresponded with today's Niche of the Pallia, objects—generally strips of cloth for making relics—were lowered through an opening in the pavement to a tiny room at the site of the tomb of St. Peter.

Above the monument stood a bronze canopy supported by four twisted columns.

The basilica had five aisles. The nave was approximately 91 meters long and was illuminated by numerous windows in the side walls and the façade. It ended in a triumphal arch and was separated from the aisles by rows of architraved columns. The roof over the nave was ridged, and on each side over the aisles it had a single slope. The ceiling was timber.

The transept, nearly 66 meters long, and the apse, richly coated with gold foil, were both lower than the central nave.

A vast rectangular atrium with inside porticoes stood before the basilica. At the center of the atrium was a bronze fountain in the shape of a pine cone. (The fountain is now in the Cortile della Pigna—the Pine-

Cone Courtyard—of the Vatican Museums.) There were rich mosaic decorations on the façade (the symbols of Christ and the Evangelists), the apse (Christ with Peter and Paul), and the triumphal arch (Constantine donating the basilica). There were also frescoes, on the walls of the nave. They contained Old and New Testament scenes and portraits of the popes.

A new, bold architectural approach permitted Gregory I (590-604) to adapt the roof of the Constantinian monument for use as an altar—the first fixed altar of the church. The floor of both the apse and the area surrounding the monument was raised by a meter and a half to create a new, raised presbytery. This not only made it possible to see the altar and the monument underneath it from the transept and the nave, but it also made it possible to open up a new chapel behind the monument and beneath the apse. It could be reached from the transept by a semi-circular corridor running along the perimeter of the apse. The chapel and the corridor, decorated during the papacy of Clement VIII, are now part of the Sacred Grottoes.

From the time of Gregory I until the middle of the fifteenth century, the alterations of

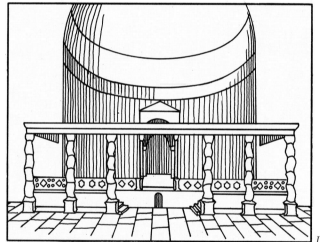

I

II

at the center of an approximately thirty-square-meter area left untouched by the family tombs that had mushroomed up all around it after the end of the first century.

There can be no doubt that this empty space, not symmetrically aligned with the mausoleums surrounding it, and the small monument, the only one of its kind in the necropolis, were the result of the will to preserve the memory of a single tomb predating the necropolis.

In the fourth century A.D., the Emperor Constantine heedlessly levelled all the necropolis mausoleums, pagan and Christian alike; and after flattening out the area surrounding them, he constructed his imposing basilica. The trophy stood in front of the

III

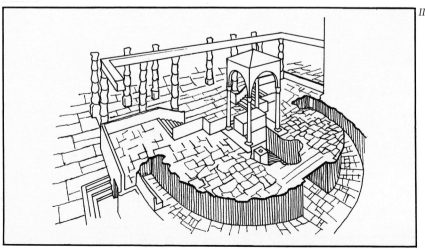

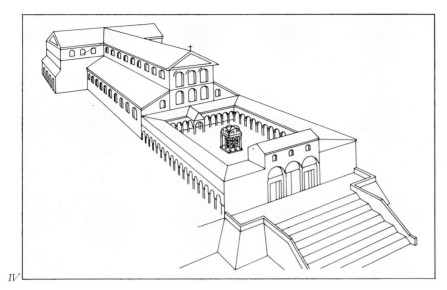

IV

V

the ancient basilica were minor. A new row of six tortile columns was set before the "monument," which was topped by a new altar; and the trophy was restructured and reduced to the present Niche of the Pallia.

With the papacy of Nicholas V, the problem of performing radical surgery on the aged, highly deteriorated building was formulated for the first time. And with his papacy there began a long period of important, but not conclusive restorations and additions—the Loggia delle Benedizioni on the outer façade of the atrium is an example of the latter. But Julius II put an end to it all in 1506 with his rash decision—equalled only by Constantine's in razing a necropolis and flattening a hill—to start the whole church over from scratch.

A century later, under Pope Paul V in 1605—fifteen years had passed since the "vaulting over" of the dome—demolition work was begun on the venerable five aisles and atrium. On May 16, 1612, the three new aisles and the façade were finished.

Only a few years earlier, Clement VIII had been forced to place a new altar, the present one, over the older altars because the basilica pavement had been raised by more than three meters. For a second time, an original architectural scheme was invented to make it possible for the faithful to approach the trophy of St. Peter: the Confessio was made into an open crypt whose pavement was level with the ancient basilica floor.

I. Reconstruction of the presbytery of the Constantinian basilica.

II. The raised presbytery after Gregory the Great's renovation at the end of the sixth century.

III. The raised presbytery with the "Confessio" and the semicircular corridor (late sixth century; the second row of columns dates from the mid eighth century).

IV. Reconstruction of the Constantinian basilica.

V. The interior of St. Peter's before the sixteenth-century reconstruction, in Raphael's fresco of the Donation of Constantine (c. 1520, Sala di Costantino).

19

19. *Statue of Pius VI in Prayer (Antonio Canova. 1822) Sacred Grottoes.*

side of the arch, who point to the words inscribed on the marble scroll above—SEPULCRUM SANCTI PETRI APOSTOLI—at once restores the atmosphere of profound worship. The Confessio is crowned by the ancient chapels underlying the four pillars of the dome; and by the elegant Chapel of St. Peter (built by Clement VIII against the back of the Constantinian altar which is now visible through a grille); and by the Irish, Polish, Lithuanian and Czechoslovakian chapels. Here, beside Peter, lie popes and kings, many of whose monuments can be admired in the church above. The Grottoes have been justly defined "a compendium of the history of Europe, from the origins to the present times." The most ancient of the tombs now accessible to the public is that of the Emperor Otto II, who died in Rome in 983 at the age of twenty-eight. The two newest tombs are the humble, unembellished sepulchre desired by Pope Paul VI and the grey marble stone with two Renaissance angels that commemorates John Paul I, whose fleeting, 33-day pontificate lived under the star of an affable, popular catechesis. The most visited tomb is unquestionably that of John XXIII, whom the people in their loving affection already see as a saint; and the most "romanticized," that of Christine of Sweden (1626-89), who renounced a Lutheran throne for Catholicism, but in exchange imposed upon Rome her court of artists and scholars—the future founders of Arcadia—said to be quite costly to the pope. For the pilgrims of the Holy Year, the most emblematic tomb is that of Boniface VIII, the pope who proclaimed the first Jubilee. It is a beautiful example of Gothic sculpure by Arnoldo di Cambio. The most effective sculptural work is the band of Renaissance reliefs inspired by triumphal Roman sculpture (possibly by Matteo del Pollaiolo) decorating the curved wall of the semicircular corridor. The most moving work is the kneeling statue of the hapless Pius VI, who died impoverished in exile and wished only to be allowed to rest as close as possible to St. Peter. He was portrayed by Canova in an attitude of remorseful piety, kneeling on a pedestal bearing the humble inscription, "Pius VI Braschi of Cesena. Pray for him."

At the exit from the Grottoes is a seated statue of St. Peter created from a Roman-age figure in a paludamentum. Although the false head and key-bearing hand give the figure a somewhat disharmonic air, it is not without a certain archaic majesty, a quality which inspired Arnolfo in his famous bronze statue for the basilica. Needless to say, it took Arnolfo's version to evoke that majesty with the authority of true art.

St. Peter's Basilica Today

When the Constantinian basilica began to show alarming signs of old age, an eminent architect of the day, the versatile Leon Battista Alberti, notified Pope Nicholas V of the fact in a now-famous technical report of 1451. Restoration was necessary. But what kind of restoration? The times had changed since the basilica had been built, and so had men's needs and tastes. The humanists' (and the learned pope's) admiration for Greek and Roman antiquity was not yet paired with a conscientious approach to conservative, "literal" restoration, nor did it allow for an equal appreciation for all ancient

20

20. Detail of the façade of St. Peter's showing the steps and the entrances to Maderno's atrium (early seventeenth century).

things, especially when those things lay outside the hallowed classical realm. Nevertheless, in the first project, by Bernardo Rossellino, for enlarging the presbytery and generally improving the edifice, the original structure was respected on the whole. Unfortunately, the death of Nicholas V brought the work to a standstill. A near half-century of conflicts, delays and indecisions led at last to the pontificate of the iron-willed Julius II, who coveted the megalomaniacal dream of erecting a colossal sepulchral monument in his own honor—he commissioned Michelangelo to do the job—adorned by forty giant statues and placed in the middle of St. Peter's church. Of course the church would have to be rebuilt entirely, but Donato Bramante had come up with a suitably triumphal plan. The project for the colossal tomb, which so obsessed Michelangelo, was never carried out. However, work was begun on Bramante's church—a Greek-cross building with arms of equal length to be surmounted by a dome ("the Pantheon set on the Basilica of Maxentius," promised the architect). The first stone was laid by the pope on April 18, 1506. It belonged to one of the four huge piers of the present-day transept. Then Julius died, in 1513, Bramante died in 1514, and the Lutheran reform came to shake the all-too-secure walls of the Vatican. Beneath the troubled eyes of Michelangelo, who had deplored Bramante's speculative building venture while as a gentle-

21

22

21. Bronze door by Filarete (Antonio Averulino, 1433-45); this is the main door of the basilica, and is opened only on special occasions; it is one of the more important early Renaissance works in Rome.

22. Detail of Filarete's bronze door showing the Judgment of St. Paul.

man he praised the plan as "clear, simple and luminous," there now passed an endless parade of projects and modifications of projects invented by a succession of superintendents of works—Raphael, Fra Giocondo, Giuliano da Sangallo, Baldassarre Peruzzi, Antonio da Sangallo. The Greek cross plan was proposed by one, the Latin cross (more functional liturgically and closer to the original) by another. In 1546 Michelangelo, old and infirm, was obliged to accept the post of director of the construction of St. Peter's much against his will. He did it for neither "reward nor profit," but only in obedience to the pope, to put an end to the wasteful squandering of the factions and, as he said, "for the glory of God, the honor of St. Peter and the salvation of my soul." Practically forced into the role of executor of his rival Bramante's architectural bequest, Michelangelo finished one of the apses of the transept to create a binding model for the others. He carefully structured the outer walls and laid the base for his dome, which was inspired by Santa Maria del Fiore of Florence as well as by the Pantheon. At the time of Michelangelo's death (1564), the dome had not progressed beyond the drum. It was continued by Pirro Ligorio and Vignola, and "vaulted" with some alterations by Giacomo Della Porta and Domenico Fontana. On April 19, 1590, the last stone was set in place. Not long afterward, however, a step that Michelangelo had always opposed was taken: the Greek cross was to be transformed into a Latin cross by extending one of the arms. The new plan would provide a roof for the whole Constantinian structure and a place for the liturgical processions dear to the Catholic Reformation. Unfortunately, the "extension" took its toll in the uncontrolled destruction of priceless treasures of art. It was built by Carlo Maderno, who also finished the façade in a

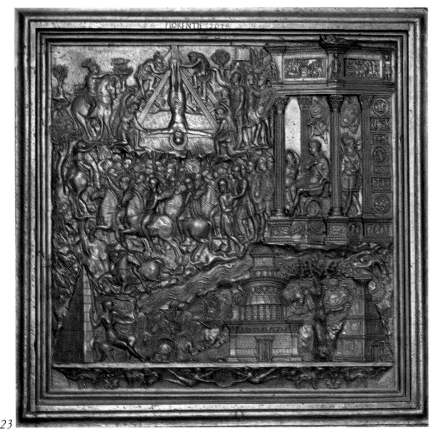

23

24

25

record five months' time. The façade was heavily criticized for its excessive width (although the preexistent structure left Maderno little choice) and because it was off-center in relation to the dome (it was centered on the obelisk). Although it lacks personality, it appears among the buildings of the Vatican complex as highly decorous. In addition, it is a fitting base for the Loggia della Benedizione from which each newly elected pope greets the crowd, and whence on major feast-days the blessing *Urbi et Orbi* is given.

The final artificer of the basilica was Gian Lorenzo Bernini. He gave the building its typically baroque air. He welded the older Renaissance portion to the later extension by his bold and clever use of natural lighting, and enriched the whole with the Baldachin and the *Gloria della Cattedra*—the Gloria reliquary with St. Peter's medieval throne—as well as with a precious tabernacle and monumental tombs. The baroque is truly the style that characterizes St. Peter's today, creating regality where there might have been redundance and fashioning the church into a grandiose, yet splendidly religious structure that neither estranges nor abases man, but exhorts him to believe fully in the greatness of his supernatural destiny.

THE PORTICO. High above three wide flights of seven steps each and a solitary stair at the top, solemnly guarded by two nineteenth-century statues of St. Peter and St. Paul, Borromini's elegant gates open on to the portico of St. Peter's, built by Carlo Maderno between 1608 and 1613.

This entrance to the supreme temple of Christianity is noble and warm, rich and yet modest; it is perfectly suited to its religious function—that of introducing the visitor to the church and preparing

23. Detail of Filarete's bronze door showing the Crucifixion of St. Peter.

24. Equestrian statue of Constantine (Gian Lorenzo Bernini, 1670), at the foot of the Monumental Staircase, at the right end of the atrium.

25. Equestrian statue of Charlemagne (Agostino Cornacchini, 1725); companion piece of the statue of Constantine, at the left end of the atrium.

The Jubilee

by Laura Draghi

Yobbel—Jubilee—was the name that the ancient Hebrews gave to the ram's horn whose blast every fifty years proclaimed a year of freedom from old bonds: debts were forgiven, slaves emancipated, and property restored to its former owners. It was only logical, then, that the name be adopted for the great year of plenary indulgence first granted by Boniface VIII in 1300 to the members of the faith who drew upon the Treasury of Merit won by Christ and the saints and demonstrated their penitence in a pilgrimage to the four apostolic basilicas of Rome—St. John Lateran, St. Peter's, Santa Maria Maggiore, and San Paolo Fuori le Mura. But the idea of the Jubilee was not a creation of Boniface. He merely sanctioned the vox popoli expressed in the rumor of a great pardon that swept through the exceptionally large crowd of pilgrims thronging St. Peter's basilica for the thirteenth centennial of the Nativity at Rome. The papal bull was transcribed on a tablet in the basilica. It announced in catchy Latin verse that "each hundredth year there will be a Jubilee in Rome." When the Curia moved to Avignon, the Romans held fast to their celebration and even insisted on shortening the interval to fifty years, after the manner of the Hebrews. But the pilgrims who came to Rome in 1350 found the throne of St. Peter empty, the city devastated by an earthquake, and the population decimated by the plague of 1348. For a century the anniversary alternated between the fifty years of the Hebrews and the thirty-three years of Christ. Sixtus IV finally settled the matter by establishing a Holy Year celebration every twenty-five years to give each generation the chance to benefit from the pardon. In 1475 the term first made its appearance in official acts and in the "printed" papers that circulated news and prayers among the faithful. In 1500 Pope Alexander VI Borgia, that far from unblemished character, acquired some merit by his attention to the liturgy and his introduction of the beautiful rite of the opening of the Holy Door, and a French Cardinal earned indulgences and fame by paying Michelangelo for his Pietà. But the traffic in indulgences carried on by shrewd Florentine bankers drew upon the church the protests of Martin Luther. Clement VII de' Medici, a pious pope, paid for it with the horrors of the "sack of Rome" only two years after his Jubilee, which itself had been saddened by the martyrdom of Thomas More, former Lord Chancellor of England and objector to the Acts of Supremacy of his King, Henry VIII. The far more austere celebration of 1550 portended the Counter

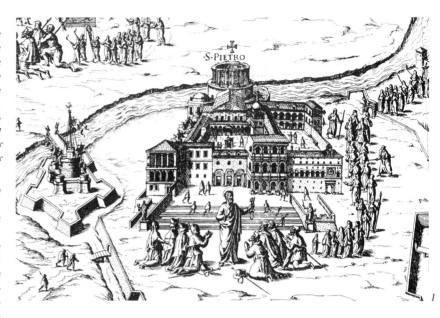

S·PIETRO

I

Reformation and witnessed the pilgrimage of Ignatius of Loyola; and while Michelangelo labored "without recompense" on the dome, Filippo Neri charitably welcomed the visiting faithful to the new Ospizio della Trinità. The Jubilee following the Council of Trent was an energetic affirmation of Catholicism. Gregory XIII exhorted the pilgrims to expiate for heretics and pagans, and as an incentive, he instituted price controls in their favor and initiated a campaign against highwaymen. The Jubilee celebrations of the seventeenth century introduced spectacular fireworks displays and outdoor lighting in the fantastic settings of Bernini and Borromini, as well as the stately processions of the Catholic sovereigns. But their new, mature emphasis on spirituality, inspired by the great mysticism of the age, which stressed humility, counterbalanced this show of magnificence. Urban VII endorsed the concept of spiritual pilgrimage for the physically incapacitated if they made compensation with acts of deep contrition. The hardship imposed by the last Jubilee of the century cut short the earthly pilgrimage of the eighty-five-year-old Clement X; and Innocent XII, aged eighty-six, did not live long enough to close the Holy Door in 1700. The Age of Enlightenment began with a conclave, the election of a sick pope, Clement XI, and a flood of the Tiber; and it proceeded to bring the Church—now a major target of the luminaries of the age—new trials and tribulations. These difficulties proved no obstacle to the success, in 1750, of the amiable Pope Benedict XV Lambertini. The brief space of three months kept Benedict from celebrating a second Jubilee, that of 1775, as its opening was delayed by a long

conclave. And though the spectre of the French Revolution hovered just outside the door, the Jubilee of that year was fervid, after the religious example of Pius VI, who was fated to die a prisoner of Napoleon. A mood of die-hard anticlericalism now waged war upon the Church. There was no Jubilee in 1800, and that of 1825 was distinguished by a memorable parade of Austrian soldiers "duly confessed and communicated" after they had stifled the Neapolitan uprisings. The "liberal" Pope Pius IX, who abolished the next Jubilee, lived just long enough to proclaim the celebration of 1875 in a bull that deplored the "great calamities of the Church and the century." The announcement was made without clamor, but the Holy Year was extended to 1876 to make it possible for the newly founded Catholic Action to undertake a dangerous pilgrimage. Placing his hopes in the force of youth within the church, the aged Leo XIII removed the bricks blocking the Holy Door in 1900 for a Jubilee dedicated to greater spirituality and consecrated to the Sacred Heart; whereas Pius XI, with a gesture of peace in 1925, reopened the Loggia of Benediction that had been scornfully closed after the Porta Pia affair. He greeted the enormous crowd below and dedicated to them a famous Missionary Exhibit in words that underlined the universal vocation of Catholicism. Peace and hope after the horror of World War II were inspired by the magnificent Jubilee of 1950, when Pius XII beatified the children Maria Goretti and Domenico Savio and proclaimed the dogma of the Assumption—two bold acts of faith in the Christian victory over death. Men of every race and creed flocked to Rome:

the ecumenical era had begun. It was reconfirmed in the Jubilee of 1975, proclaimed by Pope Paul VI at the close of a decade of political and social rebellion. His predisposition to philosophical doubt led him to confide: "We have asked ourselves whether it is worthwhile to maintain a tradition of this kind in our time." But he eventually decided in favor of an opportunity for the "spiritual renewal of man." The selfsame principle animated the special Jubilee of the Redemption (25 March 1983–22 April 1984).

I. Pilgrims in St. Peter's Square during the Holy Year of 1575, in a contemporary woodcut.

II. Boniface VIII proclaims the first jubilee in 1300 (fresco attributed to Giotto in St. John Lateran).

III. John Paul II opening the Holy Door.

IV. John Paul II entering St. Peter's through the Holy Door.

II

III

IV

26

27

26. *View of the nave: the major themes of the basilica become immediately clear from this point, just inside the doors at the center of the nave.*

27. *Holy-water stoup borne by two putti (Agostino Cornacchini, early eighteenth century), at the entrance end of the nave.*

him for its rites. Its statues and symbolic figures are, so to speak, a catechistic compendium of Catholicism in images. And justly so, for to enter the church by right, one must have received instruction in the doctrines of the faith. Even the doors that lead from the portico into the temple fulfill this initiatory function. There are five of them, flanked by six marble columns originally belonging to the Basilica of Constantine. The last to the right, the work of Vico Conforti (1950), depicts in sixteen classical panels the theme of Salvation, of which the Jubilee is part. This door is the Holy Door. It stands open only in Holy Years. At all other times it is bricked up in a wall which at the beginning of each Jubilee the pope symbolically breaks down with the silver hammer.

On the left side of the portico one may admire a magnificent equestrian statue of Charlemagne, a baroque work by Agostino Cornacchini (1725). Its companion-piece to the right is Bernini's beautiful sculptured portrait of Constantine (1670). These two historical personages stand here by right. One was the first ruler of the Holy Roman Empire, the other the first Christian emperor. They represent the "sentinels"—that is, the "secular arm" of the Church's exclusively spiritual kingdom.

The door at the center, the oldest of the five, was executed between 1440 and 1445 by the Florentine goldsmith Filarete. His skill is evident in the finely finished workmanship of the historical scenes, the figures, and the engraved mythological backgrounds and friezes, which abound in Renaissance classicism. The door to the right is by Venanzio Crocetti. It was set in place in 1964 and represents the sacraments in everyday scenes of Christian life. The corre-

28

sponding door to the left is the most recent (1977). Its theme, Good and Evil, was illustrated with a lyrical sensitivity to the major problems of the present century by Luciano Minguzzi. The last door on the left, the *Porta della Morte* (Door of Death) contains a portrait of Pope John XXIII and is the work of Giacomo Manzù (1964).

Before crossing the threshold of the main Porta dei Sacramenti, turn and notice the so-called *Mosaic of the Navicella* above the central portico gate. In it, the apostles' boat is tossed about in a stormy sea, while Christ walks on the waters and holds up a near-drowning Peter (Matthew 14, 26-33). The work was commissioned from Giotto for the atrium of the old St. Peter's in the year of the first Jubilee of 1300 by Cardinal Stefaneschi. Today the cardinal humbly stands in mantle and mitre, deep in prayer among the waves in an inconspicuous lower corner. The original was altered by a bad restoration, and the hand of Giotto is now only a faded memory. Nevertheless the underlying message of the scene is still topical for both the individual believer, who is daily faced with the challenge of faith, and the Church, which is an eternal boat beset by the storm.

THE INTERIOR. The major themes of the basilica may be seen clearly from the center of the nave, near the entrance. The straight white lines of the colored-marble pavement draw attention to the heart of St. Peter's, the *Confessio*. The word, meaning "heroic profession of faith," designates the tomb of St. Peter, magnificently placed and decorated by Carlo Maderno and Domenico Ferrabosco in 1600, and lighted by eighty-nine silver lamps whose flames visibly glow from afar. Above and beyond the Confessio stands Bernini's

29

28. View of the nave from the balcony of the dome; in the distance beneath the entrance is the famous red porphery wheel.

29. Barberini coat of arms (detail of the base of Bernini's Baldachin); Maffeo Barberini reigned under the name of Urban VIII between 1623 and 1644; the decorative scheme of St. Peter's dates from his pontificate.

30

31

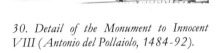

32

30. Detail of the Monument to Innocent VIII (Antonio del Pollaiolo, 1484-92).

31. Detail of the Monument to Urban VIII (Gian Lorenzo Bernini, 1647); this monument is a companion piece of the one to Paul III beneath the Throne; the triumphal redundancy typical of the baroque style reappears in most seventeenth century burial monuments after this one.

32. St. Longinus (Gian Lorenzo Bernini, 1639); one of the four statues placed in the niches of the pillars that support the dome.

33. St. Veronica (Francesco Mochi, 1639); also in a niche beneath the dome.

34. Tabernacle of the Chapel of the Holy Sacrament (Gian Lorenzo Bernini, 1675).

35. Detail of the Monument to Alexander VII (Gian Lorenzo Bernini, 1655-67).

great *Baldachin* (1633). This imposing, yet graceful structure is inspired by the ceremonial canopies of open-air processions. Animated and vibrant, it provides a solid shield over the papal altar while preserving the sense of impermanence of processional devices. At the same time it frames the basilica's most significant object, the bronze *Throne* of the apse, making it seem nearer than it really is. The throne is touched by radiant clouds and surrounded by swarms of rejoicing angels clambering among the fine bands of golden rays which shoot out from the oval window of white and yellow glass high above. In the window, the far-off image of the pentecostal dove glows like the heart of a fabulous monstrance. This throne, toward which the Holy Spirit descends, is the *Cathedra Petri*, the gigantic reliquary containing the remains of what was once, in the eyes of religious tradition, the true throne of St. Peter. It was conceived by the powerful theological imagination of Bernini, who held that the image which delights the eye is simultaneously rich food for the mind. From the same position, one may also glimpse part of the dogmatic inscription on the frieze at the base of the dome: "Thou art Peter, and upon this rock I will build my church, and the gates of Hades shall not prevail against it" (Matthew 16, 18). The confessio, the altar, and the throne are the *summa* in beauty and symbolic value of the Counter Reformation's decisive reappropriation of Peter's mandate. The Council of Trent (1563) reaffirmed "one holy, catholic" Church,

36. Detail of the Monument to Clement XIII (Antonio Canova, 1792); this was the first neoclassical sculpture to be placed in St. Peter's.

37. Detail of the Monument to Pius VII (Berthel Thorvaldsen, 1800-23); an academic but finely balanced work by a follower of Canova.

The Church of the Pope

by Annamaria Pericoli

Rome is the city of the pope; therefore, St. Peter's is the church of the pope. But the equation doesn't work the same way for everyone. Strangely enough, it is with the real Romans, i romani di Roma—that it makes the least impression.

The presence of the papacy, carved in the stones, images, literature, and customs of Rome, has shaped the culture and character of the Romans, even though today their collective memory only goes back a hundred years or so. The pope for the Romans is "one of us" in a way unlike that of other Catholics, be they Italian, American, French or German. "È rimorto il papa" (the pope's dead again) a Roman daily dared to write at the death of John Paul I. And as for St. Peter's, it is affectionately nicknamed er Cupolone (Big Dome).

One might liken Rome with its traces of history to a concerto with St. Peter's as the solo instrument. The basilica has been the "church of the pope" throughout its long, long history, although it has not meant the same thing to believers and non-believers. But not even non-believers can ignore the fact that this edifice has a special meaning deriving from its bond with the man whom Christ himself invested with the highest mission of all. That mission was to guide and to interpret the widest range of human experience, for the Christian religion is kneaded with the world as yeast is kneaded with dough.

Everything in the basilica testified to this "strategic relationship," this mixing of heaven and earth, sometimes accepted and sometimes rejected, but impossible to ignore. On the red Egyptian porphyry disk, for example, Charlemagne and many kings after him knelt before being anointed ruler by the pope. In the ancient basilica of Constantine it was closer to the presbytery. Now visitors tread on it and pass it by just inside the entrance (it was already outdated at the time of the baroque restoration). Another sign is the gold gathered here in impressive quantities and now nearly gone. It was repeatedly plundered, stolen and confiscated from the fifth century on, first by Genseric's Vandals, then by the Saracens, Lansquenets, Napoleon, and, finally, the Roman Republic of 1849. But these "sacriligious" robberies have restored to the church of the Vicar of Christ the holy inner dimension established for it by the categories divine. "Silver and gold have I none; but what I have, that I give thee," said Peter to the lame beggar at the door of the Temple Beautiful as he healed him.

Another emblematic sign is Giotto's mosaic of the Navicella now in the entrance porch (unfortunately, positioned against the light and in very poor repair). It represents a truth that every pope—even those of the darkest ages—has always kept in mind. The Lord saved the boat of the Apostles and he also saved Peter who, while wavering in his faith, wished to come to him on the waters. Hence Christ, who chose Peter as his successor and Rome as the heart of the Church, became by his act the guarantor of St. Peter's over the centuries.

The modest emblem of the Navicella was chosen as a seal by Paul VI, the pope who donated the papal tiara to the poor and placed a crucifix on the pastoral staff as a symbol of the paradox of the strength of weakness. The gestatorial chair is gone, too, now, replaced under John Paul II with the white papal jeep.

The baroque basilica of the popes, cause of the scandalous division of the Christian world, the basilica of opulent canonizations illuminated by forty thousand candles and brilliant fireworks displays, has become in the mind of today's generation simply the white basilica—white for the vestments of the bishops of the world assembled at the Second Vatican Council, which was the first ecumenical council to address itself to all the Christian churches, to the believers of every faith, and to all men of good will.

This is the church of the pope's Wednesday catechesis, given first in the basilica, then in the magnificent Audience Hall—Pier Luigi Nervi's modern addition to St. Peter's—and lastly in the enormous square, sometimes for two days running, when the crowd is too great to be held by Bernini's colonnades.

It is the church that was thronged with men of all creeds at prayer for the dying Pope

I

II

III

IV

V

John XXIII, the church of the embrace of re-conciliation between Athenagoras and Pope Paul VI, of his kiss at the feet of Melitone, of the meeting with the Primate of England.

Whereas the temporal powers of the church have diminished, its spiritual boundaries have been expanded to their original dimension, the dimension of universality and divinity that is mingled with human nature in every people and culture, and that the basilica's architectural lines, sculptures and paintings sought to represent.

I. John Paul II performing the blessing "Urbi et Orbi," from the loggia of St. Peter's on the day of his election.

II. The Mosaic of the Navicella by Giotto, executed for the jubilee of 1300; little of the original workmanship remains today.

III. The Second Vatican Council in session in St. Peter's (1965).

IV. John Paul II celebrating Mass in St. Peter's beneath Bernini's impressive Baldachin.

V. A papapl audience in Nervi's huge auditorium.

VI. The Audience Hall.

VI

38

39

40

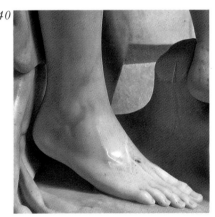

41

38-42. Pietà (Michelangelo Buonarroti, 1498-99), carved by the artist at the age of twenty-nine.

and the theme of unity recurs throughout St. Peter's in a wealth of symbols of the union of the Eastern and Western Churches. Examples are the statues of the Church fathers—the Greek St. Athanasius and St. John Chrysostom and the Roman St. Ambrose and St. Augustine—at the base of Bernini's throne, and the bilingual inscription referring to Peter as the shepherd designated by Christ for his flocks (John 21, 15-17) along the middle nave. The theme of holiness underlies the altars and chapels dedicated to the cult of the saints, the statues of the great founders of religious orders in the niches of the nave, and the medallions containing the portraits of the fifty-six canonized popes in the piers.

Thus, from the threshold onwards, one is shown the scriptural and doctrinal context of St. Peter's. This context alone provides the key to an analysis of the church.

Although it appears illusionistically to be made to the measure of man (despite its 211-meter length and its 136-meter maximum height), St. Peter's is in fact composed of oversize details. Typical examples include the tender little *Angels* of the holy water stoup that dismay the spectator with their towering two meters when seen from up close; the piers of Bramante which could contain to an inch Borromini's entire church of San Carlino; and St. Mark's pen in the mosaic of the dome, a full one-and-one-half meters long. But what

43

44

43. Gloria della Cattedra (Gian Lorenzo Bernini, 1658-66).

44. Wooden throne traditionally called the Throne of Peter (ninth century) mounted inside Bernini's Gloria; a copy is in the Treasury of St. Peter's.

45. Bernini's Baldachin (c. 1624-33).

fascinates and persuades one in St. Peter's is just this immensity, in which silent contemplation nevertheless is possible because the centripetal force of the focal points "sucks up" and minimizes all disturbing elements. The visitor will hardly notice the groups of tourists, the bustle of attendants (the famous *sampietrini*), the simultaneous performance of different religious functions and the sound of conversations in many languages. The abundant, festive, natural light, also a source of fascination, brightens the sombre, warm colors and plays with ever new effects over the golds, bronzes and marbles, investing religious ceremonies with a vivid beauty, and magically wedding the Renaissance to the baroque.

To the left of the Door of Death stands the Baptistery Chapel, the entryway of the Christian to the life of the spirit. In it, all children born in Rome may be baptized. The porphyry basin was once the cover of a sarcophagus that belonged to the Emperor Otto II. Now it is reserved for the sacrament of rebirth in Christ. Against the wall is a beautiful altarpiece, the *Baptism of Christ* by Carlo Maratta. The visitor will recognize many familiar masterpieces of painting in St. Peter's, including Raphael's sublime *Transfiguration* at the end of the left aisle. But these masterpieces are not originals—they are not

46

47

48

46. *View of the apse; at the far end is the Gloria della Cattedra.*

47. *Detail of the Throne of St. Peter showing St. Augustine (Gian Lorenzo Bernini, 1656-65); one of the four colossal statues of the Fathers of the Greek and Roman Churches, at the foot of the throne.*

48. *Gloria della Cattedra, in brilliant gold, with the dove of the Pentecost.*

even paintings. They are fine mosaics made by the Vatican School of Mosaic founded during the eighteenth century, and they were held to be suitable replacements for the more perishable paintings which, unlike mosaic, tend to lose their bright color with time.

Although painting works its charm in St. Peter's (through the medium of mosaic), sculpture triumphs there. Canova, who carved the elegant stele of the last Stuarts beside the Baptistery Chapel, is one of the more modern sculptors. But the greater part of the hsitory of the plastic arts at St. Peter's lies between Arnolfo's statue of *St. Peter Enthroned* (1300), its feet worn smooth by the countless kisses of the faithful, and two twentieth-century works: Emilio Greco's bronze bas-relief for *Pope John XXIII* and Francesco Messina's tormented portrait of *Pius XII*. Other works include a Renaissance jewel, the *Monument to Innocent VIII* by Antonio del Pollaiolo, and the ostentatious monuments of the baroque-age popes, portrayed as monarchs upon their tombs. The tombs are decorated with historical reliefs, set amidst polychrome marble draperies and flanked by buxom *Virtues*, a stylistic cliché long held in high esteem, which first en-

49

50

51

tered St. Peter's with Paul III's tomb in the presbytery. It was designed by Guglielmo Della Porta (1576) and displayed the two bold nude statues (one was later chastely dressed) of *Justice* and *Prudence*. The great baroque masters were the exuberant Bernini, his more measured rival Alessandro Algardi, Francesco Mochi, and a number of other worthy representatives of that eloquent and dramatic style. The rococo influence somewhat lightens the more pictorial than plastic monument of Marie Clementine Sobieski-Stuart; and neoclassicism dignifies with its white, aristocratic forms the *Tombs of Clement XII* and *Pius VII*, by Antonio Canova and Bertel Thorwaldsen.

Another art handsomely represented in St. Peter's is that of stucco. It appears in the two great Chapels of the Choir and the Sacrament, decorated mainly by Gian Battista Ricci. The art of wrought iron achieves its perfection in the gates of Borromini, who in the early years of the seventeenth century was a mere *manovale* or unskilled assistant in the hire of his uncle, Carlo Maderno.

But the absolute, timeless masterpiece of St. Peter's is the very first statue to welcome the visitor as he enters by the Holy Door:

49. *Bronze statue of St. Peter Enthroned (Arnolfo di Cambio, late thirteenth century).*

50. *Papal Tiara (eighteenth century, Treasury of St. Peter's).*

51. *Bronze statue of St. Peter with feast-day vestments.*

52

52. Inside of the dome (height 120 meters); the decorative mosaics are based on a design by Cavalier d'Arpino (early seventeenth century).

53. Outside of the dome (designed by Michelangelo).

Michelangelo's *Pietà*, sculpted when the artist was only twenty-four. A meritorious French cardinal commissioned it for the Jubilee of 1500. Much has been written about this sublime work of art, yet silent contemplation is probably the only road to its deepest aesthetic and spiritual meaning. One thing is certain: intellectual analysis will not explain this work. If the mournful and noble Pietà contains a mystery, it is the mystery of the incarnation, passion and death of God, borne and glorified in the Mother and Son. No other artist has been able to suggest the theme with such great purity.

THE TRANSEPT AND THE INTERIOR OF THE DOME. The basilica's vast transept opens up at the far end of the aisles. Here lies the precious confessio. Above it, Bernini's triumphal baldachin, which appears light and not overlarge from afar, suddenly reveals its full majesty. Standing before it one readily understands how Rome came to be despoiled of her most venerable ancient metals, including of the roofing of the Pantheon. They were rummaged to add to the seemingly limitless stream of molten bronze that the work required. Seen from close at hand, the twisted columns inspired by the columns of Constantine's *Memoria* exhibit a wealth of elegant, leafy olive-shoot motifs animated by swarms of Pope Barberini's famous heraldic bees and by sprightly putti—the miniatures, so to speak, of the innocent, irreverent putti that play with the tiara and the holy keys on the cornice. A joyous swell of perpetual motion enlivens the entire baldachin. The twisting columns and their coat of spiral motifs contribute to the effect and irresistibly urge the eye upward to the canopy at the top, and beyond into the bright light that shines on the golds and blues of the mosaics depicting *Paradise* in the dome. The plan and most of the designs for the mosaics were supplied by Cavalier d'Arpino in 1605.

High up in the four piers supporting the dome Bernini con-

54

54. *The drum; the cornice is adorned with*
pear-leaf festoons and supported by a series
of double columns.

structed the balconies of the relics, embellished with eight authentic
Constantinian columns. Below, he made deep niches with towering
baroque statues of the saints connected with the relics, after whom
the four piers are named. The are Saint Andrew, Saint Longinus,
Saint Helen, and the legendary Saint Veronica, who anxiously runs
in the dramatically strong wind shown blowing the veil upon which
the image of Christ appeared. Now, at last, one can admire the fine
details of the throne of St. Peter at the end of the apse, including the
relief of *Peter Receiving Pastoral Primacy*. Although Bernini used the
scene simply to decorate the back of the chair, he succeeded in giving it theological prominence by placing it strategically at the center.

THE DOME. After touring the apses and their chapels, one re-
turns toward the west end of the church. From here the ascent may
be made to the top of the dome, an experience without which no visit to St. Peter's would be complete. One hundred forty-five steps
lead up to the gallery above the crossing. The view of the transept,
the baldachin, and the dome's mosaic—with Jesus, Mary, and Saints,
rows of angels, and, at the top, God the Father—is spectacular. A second staircase leads upward between the inner and outer shells of
the dome to the terrace at the foot of the lantern (302 steps, 120
meters above the square), from which a superb view extends over
Rome to the Tyrrhenian Sea and the Alban and Sabine hills.

The most charming place for the visitor to stop and rest during
his climb is the terrace on the roof of the basilica, where the great

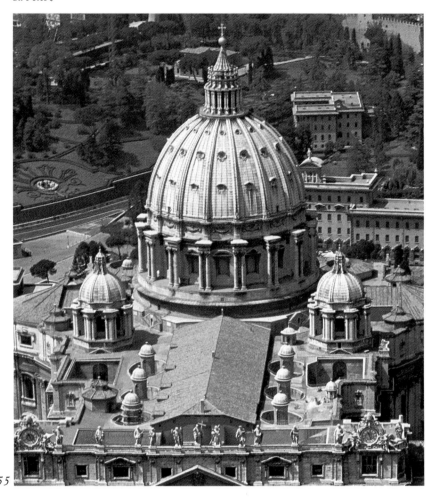

dome springs forth together with the two blind domes built for "balance" by Giacomo Della Porta and the six small oval turrets by Carlo Maderno. Here is a pensile village of undulating, broken surfaces; skylights, basins, stairways, balconies, turrets, closet shops or storerooms, and low walls and balustrades guarded by tall (six meters plus) statues of Christ, John the Baptist, and the apostles, who turn their rough-hewn, iron-bound backs on the church to keep watch over the busy square below. From here one may best contemplate the power of the "beautiful and terrible machine ... so well supplied with walls" of which Vasari admiringly speaks. One may summon feeling and memory to a leisurely analysis of the architectural details—the huge windows with alternating curved and pointed tympanums; the double columns supporting the cornice (here Michelangelo wanted to set sixteen colossal marble prophets, but found their weight prohibitive); the band of feather-light pear festoons (for Sixtus V, whose surname was Peretti); the superb vault with its powerful ribs, so wonderfully wrought by Della Porta and Fontana (with minor infidelities to Michelangelo), dotted with medallion-like windows, and surmounted by the lantern, with its crown of candelabra and the gilded ball that carries the very last word of St. Peter's Church: the cross.

55. Aerial view of the basilica showing the terrace and the minor domes.

56. Panorama of the papal palaces from the cupola; in the foreground is the roof of the Sistine Chapel, on the left the Borgia Tower.

57. The Vatican Gardens as seen from the dome; in the distance is the building that houses the Vatican Pinacoteca.

58

59

58. *Sarcophagus of Giunio Basso (fourth century A.D.), Treasury of St. Peter's; the reliefs illustrate scenes from the Bible.*

59. *Crux Vaticana (late sixth century), Treasury of St. Peter's; donated to Old St. Peter's by the Byzantine Emperor Justin II.*

The Sacristy and the Treasury

The Sacristy of St. Peter's is a "corollary" of the basilica—a necessary, yet architecturally distinct addition. The edifice was built by Carlo Marchionni in 1776-84 to give the church a real sacristy, not provided for in Michelangelo's design. The project was heavily debated and long delayed, especially because it required the sacrifice of several venerable monuments, including the mausoleum or "rotunda" tomb of the Emperor Theodosius I.

At the entrance to the sacristy stands the nineteenth-century *monument to Pius VIII*. Beyond is a corridor containing a memorial stone inscribed with the names of the 147 popes buried in St. Peter's and, at the corridor's end, a severe octagonal area with columns from Hadrian's Villa Tivoli. This area communicates with the large Sacristy of the Canons, who also have offices and private rooms in the building. An architectural curiosity is the seven-and-a-half-meter-high closet with a spiral staircase inside. It was originally built to hold the candelabra used in the liturgy. The Museum of the Treasury of St. Peter's has been housed in the west wing of the sacristy since 1974. Here, visitors will find the more important exhibits from the ancient basilica and the best of the gifts given over the ages by illustrious and munificent men of the faith—or rather what is left of them after a sad history of pillage, vandalism and confiscation (Napoleon requisitioned much of the treasure in 1807).

The Treasury tells the story of St. Peter through exhibits of widely differing periods, genres, styles and provenance. The three most famous pieces are the refined fourth-century Roman sarcopha-

60

61

62

gus with biblical scenes, created for a high official of the empire and Christian neophyte, Junius Bassus *praefectus urbis*; the colossal papal tiara made of silver, gold, precious stones and pearls, used each June 29 to crown the bronze statue of St. Peter (solemnly robed for the occasion in a magnificent cope); and the spectacular bronze tomb of Sixtus IV, dated 1493, by Antonio del Pollaiolo. In the latter work, the pope in his tiara gravely sleeps on a magnificent bier elegantly framed by fine ornaments and acanthus leaves. His head rests against two thick bronze cushions finely edged with a profusion of embroidery and softly wrinkled where he lies. All around the base, which glides into a slight curve at the bottom, are trapezoidal areas with vibrant female figures (allegories of the Liberal Arts, Philosophy and Theology), and the pope's recumbent body is accompanied on three sides by the seven Christian virtues. Nothing in this funeral monument recalls the chill and sorrow of death. The drama that it represents is calm and serene. The light plays over the vigorous surfaces and among the abundant folds of drapery, which banishes all trace of *rigor mortis* from the corpse, and with its modelling reveals harmonious virginal graces in the grand old man. The measured, regal humanism of Florence could have chosen no more beautiful form to take in the world of papal Rome.

60. Detail of the bronze Tomb of Sixtus IV (Antonio del Pollaiolo, 1493), Treasury of St. Peter's.

61. So-called Dalmatic of Charlemagne, Treasury of St. Peter's; now identified as a Byzantine masterpiece.

62. Weathercock of Old St. Peter's, Treasury of St. Peter's; it stood atop the bell tower from the eighth to the early seventeenth century.

The Roman Curia
by Francesco Margiotta Broglio

The Roman Curia was defined by the new Code of Canon Law of 1983 as the organism through which the pontiff customarily handles matters regarding the Universal Church. It therefore carries out its functions for the good and in the service of the various churches, in the name of the pope and with his authority. The Second Vatican Council had used greater precision, however, in speaking specifically of functions to be carried out in the service of the bishops, and in underscoring the new functions of pontifical offices created historically for a centralized administration of ecclesiastical affairs—an administration that required profound renewal in the spirit of collegiality and decentralization sanctioned by the ecumenical council.

The Roman Curia, reformed by Pope Paul VI in 1967 and made up of a vast group of organs with specific duties, is called "Roman" because the pope is both the bishop of Rome and the head of the Universal Church. At present it includes the Secretary of State, similar to a prime minister; the Council for Public Affairs of the Church, a sort of foreign ministry; the Sacred Congregations, ministry-like organs; the Secretariats, autonomous administrative bodies; advisory bodies such as the Lay Council and the "Justitia et Pax" Study Commission; the courts, and a number of curial offices.

The Congregations are organized into different areas of jurisdiction that range from the doctrine of the faith (offspring of the Holy Office of the Inquisition, established to fight heresy and heresiarchs) to the Catholic Churches of Eastern Rites, from the bishops to the clergy, from the sacraments to the saints, and from Catholic education and the religious orders to missionary activity for the evangelization of the peoples of the world. The Secretariats originated with the Second Vatican Council as a means of favoring dialogue between the Catholic Church and other churches, but they actually work for the union of all Christians as a means of realizing the council principles on ecumenism, and for the encounter of the Church with non-Christians and non-believers. They are agile and more highly articulated than the older Congregations which played such an important part in the last three pontificates.

The "Justitia et Pax" Commission and the Lay Council were created by Pope Paul VI in 1967 to carry out the decrees of the Second Vatican Council. The vast range of activities assigned to the Lay Council includes study and advisory functions, the promotion of the lay apostolate and the coordination of relations between the laity and the ecclesiastical hierarchy. The "Justitia et pax" Commission was meant "to stimulate the support of the Catholic community for the development of impoverished areas and the cause of social justice among nations" (Encyclical Gaudium et Spes). It has been extremely important in the peace-making efforts of the Holy See and in the development of the so-called "North-South" dialogue within the new international economic order.

The Roman tribunals are three, the Supreme Tribunal of the Apostolic Signatura, the Sacred Apostolic Penitentiaria and the Sacred Roman Rota. The Rota, with its over-six-hundred year-old traditions, is unquestionably the most famous, partly because it generally considers marriage annulment cases.

Among the curial offices (also ranked as ministries), the most ancient is undoubtedly the Apostolic Chancery, which keeps the papal seals and the so-called fisherman's ring (St. Peter fishing) used to authenticate pontifical acts. Its first head is said to have been St. Jerome. Economic matters are handled by the Prefecture of Economic Affairs of the Holy See—something like a combination of a ministry of the Budget and Audit Committee—and the Administration of the Patrimony of the Apostolic See, which manages the property of the Holy See and handles whatever other economic matters are assigned to it by the pope. The other offices are the Office of Ecclesiastical Statistics; the Prefecture of the Apostolic Palace, which makes preparations for pontifical ceremonies and regulates papal audiences and all matters regarding protocol in the pontifical courts and palaces; and the ancient Apostolic Camera, headed by the Cardinal Camerlengo (a sort of chamberlain) who fulfills his important functions especially in the period between the death of a pope and the election of his successor. The many curial offices are coordinated in various

ways by the Cardinal Secretary of State who, after the reforms of Pope Paul VI, became responsible for the general coordination of government. In a state, mutatis mutandis, his functions would belong to the head of the cabinet. Today—after the Second Vatican Council and the actuation of the abovementioned reforms—certain diocesan bishops from various parts of the Catholic world can also participate in the plenary meetings of the several Congregations.

I. A session of the Tribunale della Sacra Rota in an illuminated document from the Archivio Segreto Vaticano.

II. Bishops of the curia around the pope in a fresco by Raphael showing the Crowning of Charlemagne; the scene is set in the sixteenth century (Raphael's Stanze).

III. A meeting of the calendar reform commission under Gregory XIII in a painting of 1582 (Siena, Archivio di Stato).

II

III

63. The *Arco delle Campane* (*Arch of the Bells, here with the Swiss Guard*) is the main entrance to the Vatican City.

64. The outside of the Sacristy (*Carlo Marchionni, 1776-84*).

65. The Papal Audience Hall, with its unique roof (*Pier Luigi Nervi, 1971*).

66

67

THE VATICAN GARDENS
by Francesco Papafava

66. Elevation view of the southwest corner of the apse, part of Michelangelo's original design.

67. The apse.

The circle of walls built by Leo IV in the mid-ninth century formed the eastern bulwark of the populous suburb that grew up between the Tiber and St. Peter's, and that spread out behind the basilica, along the top of the *Mons Vaticanus*, which formed the area's western and southwestern boundary.

How the hilly area between the apse and the walls, today a garden, was organized in the Middle Ages, is unknown. It certainly was not built upon, and it probably was largely uncultivated. It may have been just this possibility of having a large garden (or more precisely, a protected cultivated area) which induced the pope to build a residence in the Vatican. For this purpose he acquired the hill, today occupied by the Cortile di San Damaso and the palace of Sixtus V, and the entire valley (which was later made over to form the Cortile del Belvedere and Cortile della Pigna) up to the outer slope of *Mons Sancti Egidi* (the hill atop which Innocent VIII would build the palazzetto del Belvedere at the end of the fifteenth century), extending the area of the Vatican to its natural boundaries on the north and northwest. To protect his new acquisitions Nicholas built a sturdy circle of walls that joined up with the fortified enceinte of Leo IV. He brought water to the area, and planted vines and fruit trees on the site of the present Belvedere and pigna courtyards. The slopes to the west remained wooded.

Nicholas V (1447-55) was the first to conceive a series of gar-

68. *The Vatican Gardens, seen with the apse and dome of St. Peter's and, on the right, part of the Palazzo del Governatorato.*

dens that would have a practical application in the ceremonies of the papal court and that would also be used for the pope's personal enjoyment. He probably extended their area to the north of the tower that he had built to protect the Porta San Pietro (which for this reason was also called the *Porta Viridaria* or Garden Gate), along the Via Francigena, the medieval road connecting Rome with the North.

A contemporary writer describes a system of large and small gardens, a fountain, a fish pool, and an enclosure for rabbits. Between the tower and the palace, in the area now occupied by the Cortile di San Damaso and the Palace of Sixtus V, lay the *hortus segretus* or private garden, the area closest to the palace, which was used for entertaining guests.

At the end of the fifteenth century a loggia was built to plans by Antonio del Pollaiolo atop the boundary walls at the north end of the gardens. The loggia, which overlooked the open country outside the walls, was called the Belvedere, and was originally conceived as a place where Innocent VIII could stop and rest during his walks. Later two small rooms were added on the east side to allow for longer stays.

In the first decade of the sixteenth century, during the papacy of Julius II, Donato Bramante realized a bold, theatrical plan for transforming the valley between the palace and the Belvedere. He made the valley over to form three stepped terraces connected by staircases. (His design would later be broken up—first by the Library of Sixtus V, and then by the Braccio Nuovo or new wing of the Mu-

69

70

69. *Fountain of the Sacrament (Giovanni Vasanzio, early seventeenth century).*

70. *Fountain of the Eagle (Giovanni Vasanzio, early seventeenth century); the eagle above the grotto is the heraldic symbol of the Borghese, the family of Paul V.*

71. *The fortifications of the Sistine Chapel.*

72. *View of the Gardens.*

seums—to form the Cortili del Belvedere, della Biblioteca, and della Pigna.) In place of Nicholas III's enclosure, Bramante built a great rectilinear defensive wall whose inner façade was elegantly adorned by superimposed blind arcades in correspondence with the covered galleries that linked the wall with the palace, bridging the various levels of the garden. The uppermost gallery (the only one which corresponds to the present Cortile della Pigna) led directly from the papal residence to the Belvedere.

During the sixteenth century the lowest terrace (today the Cortile del Belvedere) was used for plays and receptions, whereas the upper terraces, especially the present-day Cortile della Pigna, were kept as gardens and merged with the other gardens that stretched over the site today occupied by the Pinacoteca, the Giardino Quadrato, and the Pio-Clementine Museum.

The State Called Vatican City
by Francesco Margiotta Broglio

Church, Holy See, Vatican City: these three terms indicate three different things, but are often used improperly and frequently confused. In fact, most of the time it is the word "Vatican" that takes the place of the other two.

According to an ancient definition—it dates back to Giovanni Bellarmino—the church is the society of men who have been baptized, profess the Catholic faith, partake of the sacraments, and seek the same spiritual ends under the guidance of the Roman pope and the bishops. The Second Vatican Council provided further clarification: the church consists of "a single people of God rooted in all the nations of the earth."

The Holy See, on the other hand, is the central government of the Universal Church. It consists of the pope, the bodies of the "Curia Romana" through which he exercises his powers, and the other church organisms that collaborate with the pontiff. Among them are the College of Cardinals, the Synod of Bishops, and the Ecumenical councils which are convened and presided over by the pope and have legislative power over the Catholic Church. Keep in mind that as Bishop of Rome, the pope governs the individual diocese of Rome through a "cardinal vicar."

But the agreement reached with Italy in 1929 known as the Lateran Treaty (and revised in February 1984), also gives the pontiff full temporal sovereignty over the State called the Vatican City.

The popes took up their residence in the buildings erected around the basilica of St. Peter's during the later 1300s, after their return from Avignon to Rome. And they continued to live in those very same palaces after the fall of the temporal power and the annexation of Rome by Italy.

The need to resolve the "Roman Question" by guaranteeing independence for the Holy See on a formal level, through territorial sovereignty, limited though it might be, lay behind the creation of the new "State of Vatican City" with the Lateran Treaty of 1929. The preamble of this treaty, signed by Mussolini and Cardinal Gasparri on February 11, 1929 in the Palace of the Lateran, states that Italy and the Holy See decided to create the Vatican City and to recognize "the unconditional property, the exclusive and absolute power and the sovereign jurisdiction" of the Holy See over the Vatican City as a means of guaranteeing the "uncontestable sovereignty even in the international field" and the "absolute and visible independence" of the Holy See.

The boundaries of the city on the whole coincided with the Vatican gardens and palaces, in which the popes continued to reside after the annexation of Rome to Italy. They were outlined in a map accompanying the Treaty and also included St. Peter's Square, which, except during particular religious ceremonies, would continue to be kept open to the public and subject to the power of the Ita-

lian police. People residing within the limits of the Vatican City were to have the right to Vatican citizenship, and merchandise directed to the Vatican from abroad was to be exempted from customs and excise taxes while in transit across Italian State territory. The Italian government also agreed to punish crimes committed in Vatican City territory at the request of the Holy See, and directly if the perpetrator of the crime were to take refuge in Italian territory. The sentences of the Vatican City courts were to become effective in Italy through the ordinary procedures established by law for foreign court sentences. The Holy See, for its part, undertook to maintain absolute neutrality and to remain apart from international congresses for the resolution of political problems and conflicts unless the parties unanimously appealed to its mission of peace. The Lateran Treaty was accompanied by a Financial Convention which provided for the payment by the Italian government to the Holy See of 750,000,000 lire in cash and one billion lire in 5% securities.

The Vatican City, with its total area of 0.44 square kilometers, is the smallest state in the world. But its symbolic significance is far, far vaster than its physical boundaries. Its present population is about nine hundred while its government consists of a commission of cardinals and a "governorship" that exercises administrative and legislative powers.

Since the Holy See is the designated ruling

power of the Vatican City, the "Holy See" participates in international organizations (the United Nations, UNESCO, the FAO, etc.), generally with observers, and signs such documents as the concluding Act of the Helsinki Peace Conference.

I. The papal suite in St. Peter's for the celebration of the reconciliation between the Church and the State of Italy on 11 february 1929 (print based on a painting by Arturo Bianchini, Milan, Museo di Storia Contemporanea).

II. The Swiss Guard and the Palatine Guard (the latter dissolved by Paul VI) in St. Peter's Square.

III. The walls on the west side of the Vatican City; behind the wall is the Torrione di San Giovanni, part of the old medieval walls.

IV. The Palazzo del Governatorato (built in 1931), governmental and administrative center of the State of Vatican City.

V. The Vatican Railroad bridge outside the entrance to the Vatican State; in the distance, among the trees, is the Vatican Radio tower.

73. *The Gardens with the Radio Tower.*

74. *Casina of Pius IV (Pirro Ligorio and Sallustio Peruzzi, 1553-62); a gem of mannerist architecture.*

The area to the west of the Cortile del Belvedere was entirely wooded. Today trees still cover part of the zone.

New wings were soon added to the Loggia del Belvedere, which became a small palace in its own right, where artists resided. Julius III and Pius IV further enlarged and remodelled the building with a view to making it a more comfortable "retreat" for the popes. The garden enclosed by the new wings (which in the eighteenth century would become the Cortile Ottagono of the Museums) was planted with orange trees and adorned with classical statues from the papal collections, the first core of the Vatican Museums.

In 1558-65, while Pius IV was pope, Pirro Ligorio closed off Bramante's ascending terraces on the west side with a building, made of long halls, similar and parallel to the one built by Bramante, completing his structure with the Nicchione della Pigna.

Previously Paul IV had commissioned Pirro Ligorio to build a small villa in the "forest," where the pope could spend his leisure hours, as the Palazzetto del Belvedere was unsuitable for this purpose. The building, made up of an enclosed pavilion and a loggia separated by a small elliptical courtyard (with entrance niches at both ends) and sumptuously decorated with stuccoes of mythological and floral motifs, was completed during the pontificate of his successor, from whom it receives the name Casino of Pius IV.

Pius IV also planted a "Private Orange Orchard" within an elegant enclosure. Today known as the Giardino Quadrato (Square Garden), it originally included the site on which the Pinacoteca now stands.

In 1589 Sixtus V entrusted Domenico Fontana with the task of erecting an imposing new palace (today it still contains the papal apartments) opposite the medieval palace, on the site of the *hortus segretus* (Nicholas V's garden, part of which may still be seen in the Cortile di San Damaso). Sixtus also built the Library across Bramante's three ascending Belvedere terraces.

Paul V (1605-21) embellished the garden with fountains, the most impressive of which are the Fontana del Sacramento and Fontana dell'Aquilone.

From Paul's day until 1930 no substantial changes were made in the Vatican Gardens (the popes had chosen in the meantime to

make the Quirinal Palace their permanent residence). The gardens extended westward from the Belvedere and Pigna courtyards beyond the fortifications of Leo IV to the more recent walls of Nicholas III. The area between the apse of the basilica and Leo's walls—partly uncultivated, and partly planted with vegetables, vines, and fruit trees—, was excluded.

With Leo XIII, the first pope to spend his entire pontificate in the Vatican in voluntary reclusion as a result of the proclamation of Rome as the capital of Italy, the Vatican Gardens became the object of renewed attention.

Leo built a new "retreat" around the first of the two cylindrical towers built by Nicholas V on the Vatican Hill along Leo IV's walls (the villa would later host the Specola Vaticana and the Vatican Radio), on the borderline between the two green areas of the Vatican.

With the establishment of the State of the Vatican City in 1929 the division between the two areas was eliminated. The rural village that had grown up to the west of the medieval palace was torn down. The Palazzo del Governatorato, School of Mosaic, Ethiopian College, Railway Station, and Radio Station Marconi were built in the area behind the basilica. In place of the cultivated fields, a new garden was planted around the buildings. In the traditional garden the Pinacoteca was built, a new entrance to the Vatican Museums was made, and new quarters were erected for the Pontificia Accademia delle Scienze.

75. Nymphaeum of the Casina of Pius IV.

76. Accademia delle Scienze (Academy of Science; mid-nineteenth century).

77. The Gardener's Residence in the center of the Gardens; on the right is a bronze statue of Saint Peter (nineteenth century).

Building the Vatican

by Francesco Papafava

The ancient ager vaticanus—*the Vatican fields*—spread over an area that had no fixed boundaries on the trans tiberim—*in ancient times the undeveloped side of the River Tiber. The etymology of the word is uncertain. It may have come from* vaticinium *(prophecy) after a sanctuary of Cybele the remains of which were found in 1609 beneath the present façade of St. Peter's. But* Vatico *or* Vatica, *supposedly a settlement of Etruscan origins, is an equally good possibility.*

Between the end of the republic and the beginning of the empire, in this formerly swampy and practically uninhabited area, arose the great villas of the wealthier families, as well as recreational and sports facilities.

By the Constantinian era, the Vatican had become a cemetery-suburb dominated by the great hulk of Hadrian's mausoleum (Castel Sant'Angelo).

In the third decade of the fourth century, Constantine levelled a hill and earthed over the cemetery to build an imposing basilica on the site, a basilica even vaster and greater than the Cathedral of the Lateran. He built it to exalt the tomb of St. Peter who, according to tradition, was martyred during a cruel spectacle in Nero's circus in 64 or 67 A.D. and buried in the circus's vicinity.

In the early Middle Ages, the popes who exercised their office in the basilica of the Lateran occasionally visited the Vatican for religious functions. But we have no records to tells us of the buildings that served as their temporary lodgings and no news of the structures that grew up around the basilica.

By the mid-ninth century, the Vatican was on its way to becoming the one stronghold in which the popes could be sure of a safe refuge in times of need. Following a Saracen attack culminating in the sack of St. Peter's and the devastation of the city ward that had grown up between the church and the river, Leo IV (847-855) enclosed the area within strong walls grafted onto the bulwark of Hadrin's mausoleum, which was known by then as Castrum S. Angeli. Restored and modified sections of the walls of the "Città Leonina," as the fortified area was called, can still be seen today.

Three hundred years later, the first part of the present, vast complex of pontifical palaces came into being. To the north of the basilica, probably over the ruins of one of Pope Symmachus's razed buildings, Eugenius III (1145-53) erected a new palace, which Innocent III (1198-1216) enlarged and fortified with a defensive tower. From that original core, composed of the eastern hall of today's Sala Ducale and the tower containing the Niccoline Chapel, Nicholas III (1277-80), the first pope to establish his permanent residence at the Vatican, developed his project for a quadrilateral fortress-palace with a courtyard at the center (the present Cortile del Pappagallo). Pope Nicholas also extended the Leonine walls northward to the hill on which the Palazzetto del Belvedere was to arise at the end of the fifteenth century.

Nicholas III's designs were furthered by Boniface VIII (1294-1303) and were eventually completed, after over a century of general decline in the Vatican and Rome, by Pope Nicholas V (1447-55). The humanist pope also restored Leo IV's walls and the basilica of St. Peter's, and began the Vatican Library collection inaugurated little more than twenty years later by Sixtus IV and housed on the ground floor of the papal palace.

Meanwhile—from the rule of Boniface IX (1389) on—the Pontifical Palace of the Vatican beside the tomb of St. Peter had become the seat of the central government of the Roman Catholic Church.

Pope Nicholas V inaugurated two centuries of extraordinary fervor in the building

I. Historical map of the development of the Vatican

1 Necropolis
2 Constantinian Basilica
3 Present Basilica
4 Leonine Walls and Walls of Nicholas V
5 Sistine Chapel
6 Stanze of Raphael
7 Palace of Sixtus V
8 Vatican Museums
9 Entrance to the Museums
10 Governatorato
11 Audience Hall
12 Palazzo del Sant'Uffizio

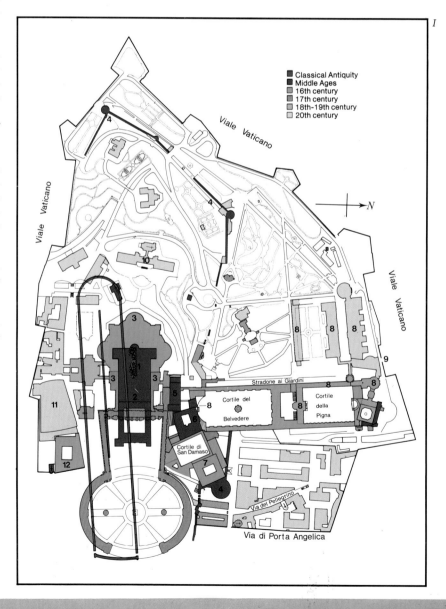

arts in the Vatican. It led to the completion of the articulated pontifical palace complex and the gigantic edifice of the new St. Peter's, and ended in the 1670s, under Pope Alexander VII, with Gian Lorenzo Bernini's arrangement of St. Peter's Square. The walls of the "Città Leonina," no longer suitable for purposes of defense, had previously been replaced on the north and north western sides of the basilica by a powerful rampart grafted onto the monumental bastion erected during the reign of Pope Paul III.

The rampart and Bernini's colonnade thenceforth defined the area of the Vatican City.

The Vatican fervor for building was rekindled for about fifty years in the 1780s. It created museums to the north and a new, convenient sacristy adjoining the basilica to the south.

For a certain period, the papal palace ceased to be used as the residence of the popes. At the end of the sixteenth century, begin- ning with Clement VIII, preference was given to the palace that Gregory XIII had built at the Quirinal as his summer residence. (Today the Quirinal Palace is the home of the President of the Italian Republic.) The return of the popes to the Vatican dates from 1870, when Rome became the capital of Italy.

After 1929, to meet the requirements of the Holy See and the tiny sovereign State that came into being with the Lateran Treaty, intense urbanization projects were carried out in the areas to the north of St. Peter's Square and to the south and southwest of the basilica. The last edifice to be built was the Audience Hall, located at the extreme southern boundary of the Vatican City and inaugurated by Pope Paul VI in 1971.

An underground building program was begun earlier, with Pope John XXIII, to avoid the further erosion of Vatican Garden space. It commenced with a structure destined to serve the Historical Museum and erected beneath the Giardino Quadrato opposite the Pinacoteca. During the present papacy, a vast building for the Secret Archives was erected beneath the Cortile della Pigna, and a similar underground building was constructed for the Vatican Library below the Library Courtyard.

II. The Vatican in a fresco by Benozzo Gozzoli of 1465 (church of Sant'Agostino, San Gimignano).

III. The Vatican in the late sixteenth century, in a detail of Ignazio Danti's map of Rome (Gallery of Maps).

IV. The Cortile del Belvedere around the mid-sixteenth century in a fresco by Prospero Fontana (Sala dei Festoni, Castel Sant'Angelo).

II

III

IV
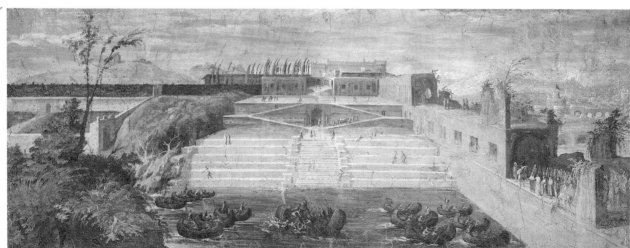

78

78. *Bronze door (1618) leading to Constantine's Portico and hence to the Vatican Palaces.*

THE VATICAN MUSEUMS
by Lucia Cecchi

The vast Vatican Museums complex is made up of the medieval apartments of the first papal residence, erected between the mid-twelfth and the fifteenth century, the fifteenth-century Sistine Chapel, and a number of other structures built around the Belvedere Courtyard and the Courtyard of the Pigna and housing the museums established by the popes in the course of the centuries.

The Papal Palace

The Vatican did not become the permanent residence of the popes until Nicholas III settled there in the thirteenth century. It was he who began the construction of a new palace—a quadrilateral structure with corner towers, left unfinished—which incorporated the edifice first built by Eugene III and later enlarged by Innocent III. He also purchased the vineyards that extended northward to the hill on which the Palazzetto del Belvedere arose two centuries later.

In the years following Nicholas III, few building projects were undertaken in the Vatican. It took Nicholas V, the humanist pope, to give a new impulse to architecture and conceive in the new Renaissance spirit a plan for transforming the ancient medieval fortress-palace into a typically Renaissance residence. Although work then executed on the palace exterior provided little to distinguish it from the grim, earlier structures, the rooms of the interior, richly decorated and sized to the Florentine notion of the "measure of man," were clear enough evidence of the revised, humanistic version of the building desired by the pope. Both Nicholas V and his successor Sixtus IV little by little carried out with their additions to the palace the building plan originally conceived by Nicholas III.

They proceeded gradually to give body to the old project for a complex of buildings positioned around the Courtyard of the Pappagallo and defended by four corner towers. To the two towers already standing, the bastion-like Sistine Chapel was added. A fourth tower was later erected by Alexander VI and named the Borgia Tower after him.

With Sixtus IV's successor, Pope Innocent VIII, the Vatican building complex first began to spread beyond its original core. In 1484 construction work was started on the Palazzetto del Belvedere, high upon a hill which dominated the countryside surrounding Rome. Conceived initially as a simple covered gallery for the leisurely walks of the pope, the palazzetto was designed by the painter Antonio del Pollaiolo and carried out by Jacopo da Pietrasanta because, as Vasari said, Antonio had no great experience in such work. Fifteen years later, the courtyard of the Palazzetto (which received its name, Giardino degli Aranci, from the orange trees that grew there), was used by Pope Julius II as the setting for the masterpieces of classical sculpture which he had collected. This was the beginning of the Vatican Museums. Bramante's project for two long, parallel galleries connecting the Villa Belvedere with the papal palace, and for the transformation of the valley between the two buildings into a colos-

79

sal courtyard with three sloping terraces linked by monumental stairways also dates from the pontificate of Julius II (1503-13). Bramante built only the eastern gallery, but his project was part of Julius II's grand scheme (too ambitious to be carried out in his lifetime) for the complete renovation of the Vatican papal residence with an increase in both decoration and prestige.

Julius II also entrusted Bramante with the task of reconstructing the side of the papal palace that faces Rome. The architect added two stories of arcaded loggias to the medieval face of the building; the third and last loggia, a trabeated peristyle, was built by Raphael during the pontificate of Leo X. Raphael succeeded Bramante in the office of chief architect to the pope, upon Bramante's recommendation. The loggias are decorated with frescoes and stuccoes combining religious themes with profane subjects drawn from the figurative repertoire of classical antiquity, carried out by Raphael's pupils, who worked under the master's direction from his drawings. The decoration reflects the antiquarian tastes of the patron, who placed his private collection of ancient statues in the third loggia, which was closed off and reserved for his private use. During the papacy of Paul III (1534-49), Antonio da Sangallo the younger carried out the renovation of the oldest wing of the papal residence, which included the *Sala Ducale* and the *Sala Regia*. He gave the palace a new, monumental entrance (the Scala del Maresciallo) and a new chapel, later frescoed by Michelangelo (the Pauline Chapel).

In the years that followed, the architects Baldassarre Peruzzi, Jacopo Vignola, and Pirro Ligorio took turns as superintendent of the

79. Cortile del Belvedere, the north side of the medieval palace.

80

80. Sala Ducale (Antonio da Sangallo, early sixteenth century); at the far end is the theatrical entrance to the Sala Regia.

81. The sixteenth-century part of the medieval palace with the Loggias, as seen from the Cortile di San Damaso.

Vatican building works and completed the projects that their predecessors had left unfinished.

It was Pirro Ligorio, summoned by Pius IV, who built the west gallery of the Belvedere Courtyard, thereby completing Bramante's project. But the immense courtyard was later cut into two nearly equal parts by Domenica Fontana, to make space for the new quarters of the Vatican Library, commissioned by Sixtus V. The latter artist and pope are also responsible for the monumental edifice that stands opposite the medieval palace and serves as the present residence of the pope.

In the seventeenth century, the medieval palace again became the object of a great building project, the Ceremonial Staircase or *Scala Regia* that Gian Lorenzo Bernini designed, as a consequence of the reorganization of St. Peter's Square, for Alexander VII.

The House of the Pope
by *Annamaria Pericoli*

Tourists rarely forego a climb up to the Dome of St. Peter's, the great hemisphere visible from every part of Rome and the outlying countryside. The dome's sweeping panorama encompasses the richest and most magnificent historical monuments in the world, adding yet another attraction to the basilica's own beauty and excellence.

Below the dome the buildings of the smallest state in the world, enclosed by a circle of ramparts, spread out on all sides. To the left of St. Peter's Square, enmeshed in a network of roofs and courtyards, is the Apostolic Palace, residence of the pope. Its severe Franciscan roofs cover the treasures of seven centuries of art: marble stairways, gilded thrones, statues, frescoes, precious paintings. The original nucleus of medieval buildings—two powerful quadrilateral structures joined by a porticoed central block and positioned alongside the Sistine Chapel and the Borgia Tower, its bastions to the west—stands face to face with the palace, on St. Peter's Square, erected by Domenico Fontana in the 1580s for Pope Sixtus V.

The splendor of the papal palace reached its peak in the days of the Renaissance, when the religious mind rejected the bare, rough-hewn forms of the Middle Ages and sought self-expression in formal perfection and in a sumptuous, magnificent, triumphal building style.

Today the top story of the medieval palace is the headquarters of the Secretary of State, and the apartments below belong to the Vatican Museums.

The pope's apartments are located in the Palace of Sixtus V. The official portion, the Audience Halls, occupies the second floor. The suite of thirteen rooms includes the majestic, richly decorated Clementine Hall; the pope's Antechamber, the Throne and Monstrance Halls, and the Library, arranged in a crescendo of importance and secrecy and penetrated in centuries past only by illustrious personages and the upper echelons of the social hierarchy—ambassadors, heads of state, high prelates and kings.

Previously, pilgrims were not allowed beyond the Clementine Hall. There, in the 1800s, the pope celebrated in their presence, as a sign of humility, the rite of washing the feet of the poor on Holy Thursday.

The Antechamber, where the visitor presented his credentials for admission to the rooms beyond, opened onto another important hall, the Hall of the Consistory. Here the pope assembled the Sacred College of Cardinals.

From 1870 to 1929—from the end of the Church's temporal power to the making of peace between the Vatican and the Italian State—the pope was a virtual prisoner in his palaces.

During the fascist period, the secret halls of the Vatican palaces hid many victims of political persecution and Jews wanted for extermination in the camps.

The open atmosphere of the postwar years, the era of the Second Vatican Council, has brought a world of changes in the Vatican as elsewhere. The rich purple tapestries have disappeared from the palace halls, the unremovable gilding seems to have diminished, the decor has been simplified.

I

II

Pope Paul VI abolished the honorary posts which bound the Roman aristocracy to papal court functions. Various articles of protocol fell. John Paul II ceased to use the ancient, royal "we."

The Library of Audiences was opened to a series of unusual guests, from the daughter of Nikita Krushchev to the Polish "Solidarity" union leader, Lech Walesa.

The third floor of the palace, which houses the pope's private apartments with his personal study and chapel, has increasingly lost its secrecy. Many audiences have been supplanted by less formal working-dinners or lunches.

The invasive television camera has penetrated even the private rooms of the pope, and his library becomes an improvised TV studio when he issues messages and encyclicals. Even the table talk seeps out: Pope John breakfasts on coffee with milk and an apple; Pope John Paul II serves a spinach ring at dinner with President Pertini.

The palace no longer shelters the pope. He, too, stands exposed to the violence of the times. Pope Paul VI was assailed in Manila in 1970. John Paul II withstood two attacks, one during an audience in St. Peter's Square in 1981 and another at Fatima a year later.

It is said of the pope that once he lived like a king, later like a prisoner, and now as he likes. But the spiritual guidance of millions of men and women and the very destiny of mankind weigh more and more heavily upon him. Constantly watched, touched by the crowds, venerated and criticized as he is, the pope still lives in "solitude" as few men do today—even if a photographer high on the dome can catch him in his private walks on the secluded balconies atop the Apostolic Palace.

I. The pope recites the Angelus before the faithful from his private apartment in the Palace of Sixtus V.

II. The recital of the Angelus takes place every Sunday at noon.

III. The Sala Clementina, antechamber of the pope's offices.

IV. The Throne Room, where the pope receives personalities and heads of state.

V. The papal library, often used for the pope's private audiences.

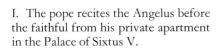

82

84

83

85

82. Pauline Chapel, detail of the Crucifixion of St. Peter.

83. Pauline Chapel, detail of the Conversion of Saul.

84. Crucifixion of St. Peter (Michelangelo, 1542-50).

85. Conversion of Saul.

86

87

The Chapel of Nicholas V

In the mid-fifteenth century, soon after his election, Nicholas V commissioned Fra Angelico to decorate his private chapel, now named the Chapel of Nicholas V after him. The frescoes were executed by Fra Angelico in collaboration with Benozzo Gozzoli and other assistants between 1447 and 1451, and illustrate the *Life of St. Stephen*, the protomartyr stoned to death in 36 A.D., and the *Life of St. Lawrence*, martyred in 258. By celebrating primitive Christianity, the frescoes reaffirmed the authority of the Roman Church. The episodes are narrated in the new figurative language created in Florence early in the century. The scenes are composed in accordance with the golden rule of proportion and the new Renaissance theory of perspective. The architecture is inspired by the monuments of ancient Rome in an ideal as well as a formal recovery of the classical world. Painting here is conceived as a cognitive experience. It searches out reality and by this means tends to the knowledge of God.

The Renaissance spirit in Fra Angelico's painting paralleled the cultural program of Nicholas V and translated the pope's ideas into the language of art. Culture and art provided access to the know-

86. Interior of the Chapel of Nicholas V, with the Stories of St. Stephen and St. Lawrence by Fra Angelico.

87. Detail of the decoration of the Chapel of Nicholas V (Fra Angelico, 1447-51); St. Sixtus (portrayed as Nicholas V) gives St. Lawrence the treasures of the church.

88

88. *The Giving of the Keys (Pietro Perugino); the frescoes at he sides were executed between 1481 and 1483.*

89. *The Punishment of Core, Datan and Abiron (Sandro Botticelli).*

90. *Detail of Moses and the Daughters of Jethro (Sandro Botticelli).*

91. *Detail of the Testament and Death of Moses (Luca Signorelli).*

ledge of God as well as consolidating Church authority. The age of classical antiquity was an exemplary age, the perfect model for the newly developing civilization of the Renaissance. This body of thought also inspired the successors of Nicholas V in their patronage of the arts. It was in this spirit that the Vatican collections, a new Renaissance institution, was founded.

The Sistine Chapel

In 1475, Pope Sixtus IV ordered the construction of a new chapel. The Sistine Chapel arose on the site of a former chapel of the thirteenth-century palace, in a building erected by Giovannino de' Dolci after a design by the Florentine architect, Baccio Pontelli. In accordance with the pontiff's desires, it had a double function: It was the defensive avantcorps of the palace (its original purpose is still evident in the military appearance of the exterior) as well as the official palace chapel. The most important humanist painters—Perugino, Pinturicchio, Luca Signorelli, Sandro Botticelli, Domenico Ghirlandaio and Cosimo Rosselli—were summoned from Umbria and Florence to fresco its walls. The chapel is a large rectangular hall whose dimensions correspond to those of the Temple of Solomon as described in the Bible: 40.23 meters in length and 13.41 meters in width.

The architecture thus foreshows the themes of the pictorial decoration. The frescoes are parallel illustrations of stories from the Old and New Testaments. Episodes from the life of Moses face episodes from the life of Christ across the room in a presentation that shows the former to be the prefiguration of the latter. Thus, the *Circumcision of Moses' Son* corresponds to the *Baptism of Christ*,

89

90

91

93

94

95

96

92

97

Moses Receiving the Table of the Law to the *Sermon on the Mount*, the *Testament of Moses* to the *Last Supper*, and so on. Above the two cycles is a gallery with the portraits of the early popes. The decorative work as a whole contains a message which is made explicit in the episode of *Christ Giving the Keys to Peter.* In the illustration of the symbolic gesture used by Christ in transmitting his authority to Peter, the Roman Church commemorates its origins and demonstrates the legitimacy of its power. The Church is the repository of the heritage of the Old and New Testaments, and the pope is successor of Moses and Christ.

In accordance with the fifteenth-century decorative scheme, the Sistine ceiling was originally painted with a simple, star-studded sky, which permitted the spectator to concentrate exclusively on the wall frescoes. Julius II decided to enrich the ceiling decoration, and in 1508 called Michelangelo in to paint frescoes of the apostles in the corbels of the lunettes. How the majestic design with episodes from Genesis evolved from the pope's initial, modest program is unknown.

The theme of the wall frescoes was resumed in the ceiling cycle, begun on May 10 of the same year. The narration works back to the story of mankind before the delivery of the divine law on Mount Sinai and the coming of Christ. It shows man's temptation and fall and tells how he awaited the Messiah, whose act of redemption healed the wound of original sin. At the center of the ceiling are the

92. *The Sistine Chapel ceiling (Michelangelo, 1509-12).*

93. *The Prophet Zachariah.*

94. *The Erythrean Sybil.*

95. *The Prophet Isaiah.*

96. *The Cumean Sybil.*

97. *The Creation of the Stars and Plants, detail of the Creator, Sistine Ceiling (Michelangelo, 1508-1512).*

98. *The Creation of Adam (Michelangelo).*

99. *Detail of the Creation of Adam.*

100. *The Original Sin (Michelangelo).*

101. *Detail of the Original Sin.*

98

99

100

101

102

103

Creation, Temptation, Explusion from Paradise, Flood, and *Sacrifice of Noah*. Between these scenes and the fifteenth-century frescoes are the *Ignudi* (nude figures probably symbolizing a pagan world that knew Revelation by intuition without in any way participating in it), the *Sybils* and *Prophets* (seers who anounced the coming of the Messiah to Israel and the pagan world), the *Ancestors of Christ* (the people of Israel awaiting Jesus), and the *Miraculous Deliverance of Israel* (the prefiguration of Christ's act of redemption).

Observing the stories from Genesis in the order of their execution, which is diametrically opposed to that of their occurance in the Bible, one notices that the crowded scenes of the *Flood* and the *Drunkenness* and *Sacrifice of Noah* give way to simpler illustrations with larger figures, culminating in the gigantic form of the Creator in the *Separation of Light from Darkness*. The divine "first appears in the imperfect form of man imprisoned by the body (Noah), and progresses to increasingly perfect forms until it becomes a cosmic being," as Charles de Tolnay points out. The narrative works its way back from the era of earthly history, in which innocence and sin alternate in the drama of everyday life, to the days of the biblical progenitors—the period of man's most direct contact with God—concluding with the portrait of the Creator. This interpretation of Genesis symbolizes the soul rising from the foundations of Hebrew and Christian thought to an intuition of the divine. The two wall cycles thus lead up to the ceiling fresco both materially and spiritually.

The ceiling decoration was finished for All Saints Day of 1512 and was inaugurated by Julius II with a solemn mass. In 1533, only a few months before his death, Clement VII commissioned Michelangelo to fresco the altar wall of the chapel with the *Last Judgment*.

But the pope did not live to see the finished work, begun in 1536 and completed under his successor, Paul III Farnese. Twenty-four years had passed since the ceiling frescoes had first been revealed to the public, and those years had thoroughly transformed papal Rome. The Protestant Reformation had opened up an irremediable breach in the Christian world. The "Sack of Rome" of 1527 had ended the myth of immunity for the city of the popes. These events had tarnished the image, built up by Julius II and Leo X, of Rome as the center of Christianity, fulcrum of Renaissance civilization, heir to the glory of ancient Rome, and maker of modern culture. Michelangelo's *Last Judgment* bears signs of this loss of the former climate of serenity, trust, and optimism in Rome. The fresco is totally lacking in perspective order—there is no "center," no "point of reference." In this space without order, a swirling crowd of figures rises and falls in a vortex around the ineluctable gesture of Christ the Judge. This gesture is the source of the movement pervading the composition, for it is the act with which divine justice is carried out. God alone judges and knows the reasons for his judgments. The tragic destiny of mankind lies in the fatality of the execution. If one recalls the fifteenth-century frescoes (particularly that of *Christ Giving the Keys to Peter*) and their rational perspective, orderly placement of figures, and underlying message, that orderly, comforting vision of the world seems to disintegrate in the whirlwind of the *Last Judgment*. In the formal and conceptual gap that separates the two paintings lies the end of the Renaissance era and the opening up of a new consciousness, born of the contemporary crisis of values.

102. *Detail of the Flood (Michelangelo).*

103. *Detail of the Flood.*

104. *The Drunkenness of Noah (Michelangelo).*

105. *The Prophet Joel (Michelangelo); painting and sculpture are joined together in a single monumental vision.*

106. *The Delphic Sibyl (Michelangelo).*

107. *One of the so-called "Ignudi" (Michelangelo).*

108. *Spandrel with David and Goliath (Michelangelo); the paintings in the corners were probably the last to be executed.*

109. *Spandrel with Judith (Michelangelo)*

108

109

110

110. The Last Judgment (Michelangelo, 1536-41); one of the greater masterpieces of the Renaissance, which foreshadows its crisis. The figure of Christ the Judge functions as the limit and focal point of the movement in this scene.

111. Detail of the Last Judgment, showing Christ in Judgment and the Virgin.

112. Detail of the Last Judgment showing Charon pushing the damned out of the boat.

111

112

113

113. *Detail of the decoration of the Sala delle Arti Liberali, Borgia Apartments (Pinturicchio, 1492-95).*

The Borgia Apartments

The apartments of Pope Alexander VI Borgia occupy the entire first floor of the papal palace, from the wing of Nicholas III to that of Nicholas V, and extend all the way to the rooms of the tower which the Borgia pope had built for himself. In these apartments—which now house the Collection of Modern Religious Art founded by Pope Paul VI in 1973—the pontiff fitted out his residence, which because of its private character was referred to as the "secret rooms." Five of these rooms were frescoed by Pinturicchio and his assistants between 1492 and 1494. In the lunettes of the first room, called the Room of the Sybils, these seers of the pagan era are paired with Old Testament Prophets. In the next room, the Room of the Credo, *Prophets and Apostles* are set side by side. Next come the *Liberal Arts* enthroned, accompanied by their devotees. The Room of the Saints contains illustrations of episodes from the lives of Christian saints. On the ceiling and the frieze of the arch is the myth of *Io-Isis* (the Greek princess who was loved by Jove and who later became queen of Egypt) and *Osiris* (her husband the king of Egypt, who after death was transformed into a divine animal, Apis the bull).

The last room, the so-called Room of the Mysteries, has representations of major events of the Christian faith.

The reason for the presence in the apartments of the myth of Isis and Osiris was genealogical. (It appears even more clearly in the omnipresence of the Borgia coat of arms with the bull in the apartment decoration). Alexander VI wished to link up his family ancestry with

114

Apis the bull, the incarnation of King Osiris, a just and benevolent sovereign worshipped by the Egyptians as a divinity. But beyond the pontiff's personal desire to add luster to his house, his choice—guided by a learned humanist of the court—reflects the great interest and respect that the Renaissance had for ancient Egyptian culture. The ancient Egyptians were considered to be the masters of the Greeks and the Hebrews, and the original source of all human knowledge. In fact, the many subjects illustrated in the Borgia rooms seem to be held together by a single theme, that of the history of mankind: the story of the continuity of the pagan and Christian worlds as it developed through various epochs and different cultures. Threaded into this theme is an awareness of the intellectual dignity of the Arts and Sciences, which are seen as age-old instruments of Revelation, from the Sybils to the Prophets and Apostles (representatives of classical antiquity and the Old and the New Testaments); from Io to Isis (the Greek maiden and Egyptian queen, who establishes a link between Hellenic and Egyptian culture); from Egypt to Israel (personified by Isis, who taught her people the alphabet and the use of hieroglyphics, and by Moses, the inventor of the Hebrew script, pictured beside her); and finally, from Egypt to the new Christian faith (Isis, like the Sybils, was believed to be a prophetic figure, a herald of the coming of Christ).

114. The Disputa of St. Catherine (Pinturicchio), Sala dei Santi, Borgia Apartments.

115

116

115. *Detail of the School of Athens, Stanza della Segnatura, showing Plato and Aristotle.*

116. *The Stanza della Segnatura, with Raphael's paintings (1509-10).*

The Stanze of Raphael

In 1507, Julius II transferred his private residence from the first floor Borgia Apartments to the second story of the papal palace. The decoration of the new rooms (*stanze*) was entrusted to Raphael, who with his assistants began working on the frescoes in 1508. The commission marked the start of the extraordinary career of the then extremely young painter, who was far from being as well known as the other artists at work for the papal court. Nevertheless the works of the others were sacrificed almost in their entirety to make space for the new frescoes of Raphael.

The first room to be frescoed (1508-11) was the Stanza della Segnatura. An iconographical scheme very common in Raphael's day was used in its decoration. The closest example is found in the Room of the Liberal Arts of the Borgia Apartments, where the personified Arts are accompanied by their devotees. Compositional schemes of this type—in which the Arts, Virtues, or personifications of other abstract concepts were surrounded by figures representing devotees or concrete examples—originated in the conviction that the things of this earth are the more or less imperfect embodiment of "ideas" or eternal principles. Thus, in four roundels of the ceiling of the Stanza della Segnatura appear enthroned allegorical figures representing *Philosophy* and *Theology* (that is, natural and revealed Truth), *Poetry* (Beauty), and *Justice* (Goodness). The great scenes below exemplify the themes of the ceiling. Corresponding to philosophy is the fresco now known as the *School of Athens*, with a large company of scholars and philosophers gathered around the figures

117

of Plato and Aristotle. Theology—the "knowledge of things divine," as the inscription on the tablet held up by the putti explains—is exemplified in the so-called *Disputa del Sacramento*, also called the *Triumph of Faith in the Eucharist*. The *Disputa* expresses the idea that the knowledge of things divine descended to earth with the Incarnation. Below the reign of heaven is the Host on the altar, and surrounding the altar, the Fathers of the Church with their inspired writings. Justice is embodied in two distinct episodes—*Justinian Receiving the Pandects*, or civil law, and *Gregory IX Approving the Decretals*, or canon law. Poetry is represented by *Parnassus*, in which contemporary and ancient poets surround Apollo and the Muses.

The continuity between ancient and Christian thought and the dignity of all the intellectual disciplines reappear as themes in this room. "The knowledge of the philosophers is seen not as inferior to Revelation, but as adding something to it. Poetry is considered to be one of the highest powers of the human spirit [*numine afflatur*, "of divine inspiration," is inscribed on the tablet accompanying the scene]. Law, or Justice . . . is put on the level that Plato claimed for it, at the very top of the hierarchy of moral values" (André Chastel). Illustrious men of present and past appear side by side here, because in this figurative interpretation of history all human experience has become contemporaneous as a result of the union between antiquity and the spiritual world of Christianity. This may well be the image of Julius II's aspiration to a universal order centered on papal, Christian Rome "reborn" to the grandeur of ancient Rome.

Julius II desired for the Room of Heliodorus a representation of the miraculous acts performed by God to defend his Church which

118. *The Expulsion of Heliodorus from the Temple, Stanza di Eliodoro; the frescoes in this room date from 1512-14.*

would affirm the legitimacy of the pontifical authority willed and protected by the Lord. The episodes represented commemorate God's protection of the faith (in the *Mass of Bolsena*), the pope (in the *Liberation of St. Peter*), the See (in *St. Leo the Great Stopping Attila*) and the patrimony (in the *Expulsion of Heliodorus*). Julius II and his suite are portrayed in both the *Mass of Bolsena* and the *Expulsion of Heliodorus* as witnesses to the miraculous events. By this means, the episodes of the past were projected into the present with the full weight of their meaning. Although no contemporaries appeared in the *Liberation of St. Peter* to symbolize a repetition of the ancient event in the present, the narrative method provided contemporary atmosphere. It used the intensity of light "to strike in a flash both the senses and the intellect" (Giulio Carlo Argan).

The Stanza della Segnatura was the only room to be completed during the pontificate of Julius II. The decoration of the Room of Heliodorus, begun in 1512, was finished in 1514, a year after the pontiff's death. The frescoes of the Room of the Fire in the Borgo were executed during the reign of Leo X. They paid him homage by illustrating episodes from the life of two earlier popes named Leo, Leo III and Leo IV. Raphael supplied the designs and some of the cartoons, but he entrusted the execution of the paintings to Giulio Romano and Francesco Penni.

The Room of Constantine was decorated between 1517 and 1524 by the school of Raphael. Most of the work was done after the master's death in 1520. Here the historical-commemorative cycle of the Room of Heliodorus was resumed in the narration of episodes from the life of Constantine. Especially significant are the victory over paganism, represented in the *Battle at Milvian Bridge*, and the establishment of the Church at Rome, illustrated in the *Donation of Constantine*.

119

120

121

119. *The Mass at Bolsena, Stanza di Eliodoro.*

120. *Detail of the Liberation of St. Peter, Stanza di Eliodoro.*

121. *The Loggia of Raphael (decorated 1517-19).*

The Pope and Art
by Francesco Papafava

The Primitive Church was long hostile to the practice of religious art. The adoration of sacred images in human guise was considered idolatry, a typical prerogative of the pagan religions. But the members of the church were steeped in the customs of their times. And as early as the second century, the faithful and even the presbyters could not keep from picturing, at least symbolically, the divinity and the hope of resurrection with the images described by Jesus himself in his parables; and eventually, in the third century, with episodes narrated in the Bible.

At the end of the sixth century, after long diatribes and occasional bloody conflicts, St. Gregory the Great claimed for art the task of spreading the faith. Images were to have a didactic function and to take the place of writing for the illiterate. Art performed this task during the Middle Ages, when the cultural traditions of the past, both iconographical and written, were preserved within the walls of Rome, the monasteries and the bishops' palaces.

At the dawn of the Modern Age, Rome was on its way to becoming the international art capital. When Martin V commenced several important restoration projects, he assigned to works of art a decorative and aesthetic role. They were to beautify the city, exalt the splendor of the papacy and glorify the church. But it was Tommaso Perentucelli, the man of learning crowned pope in 1447 under the name of Nicholas V, who with lucidity and determination pressed classical humanistic culture into the service of papal authority. He called artists and scholars to his court, saying "We venerate men of science, for they are the repositories of the eternal truths on earth." This conviction was to animate the patronage of his successors for the next hundred years.

Renaissance Rome founded its role not only on the charismatic authority deriving from the seat of the Vicar of Christ, but also on an awareness of its historical roots in imperial Rome. For the Renaissance popes, Greco-Roman art was the unsurpassed example of the highest achievement of human creativity, and human creativity was the copy of divine creativity. It followed that the beauty apparent in ancient and contemporary works of art stood for transcendental truth, and that the ideal representation of man simulated the power of God in creation. For the Renaissance popes, classical art prefigured Christian truth.

By the middle of the sixteenth century, that extraordinary and even revolutionary intellectual climate had vanished. In the austere religious environment of the early Counter Reformation, Pope Pius V, in speaking of the collection of classical sculpture in the Vatican, was able to declare that it was unseemly "to have such idols in the house." The papacy later mitigated his pious intransigence by taking care to "subordinate the monuments of impiety to the Cross" (Sixtus V) and ruling that the study of the classics must be wedded to the strict observance of Catholic doctrine. 'Religioni ac bonis artibus' reads the dedicatory inscription on the façade of the Collegio Romano, the most important scholastic institution of its day, founded in those years. Artists were called upon to exalt the Christian religion with edifying images and to celebrate the church with triumphal illustrations. Works of art were commissioned to inspire devotion and admiration.

Those severe pontiffs nevertheless must be credited with promoting by their inflexible restoration of Catholic instruction the recovery of the entire figurative patrimony of Christianity (the medieval period included), as in it lay evidence of the continuity of a nearly two-thousand-year-old spiritual tradition, and of the indestructible "primacy" of the world's most long-lived organism.

In the seventeenth century, art-collecting

I

I. The flourishing of art and science at the papal court during the early Renaissance is symbolically celebrated in this fresco by Pinturicchio representing Grammar (Borgia Apartment).

II. The revival of classical and naturalistic styles in Raphael's Parnassus (Stanza della Segnatura).

III. A Counter Reformation illustration of Sixtus V's celebrated phrase: "subjugate the monuments of impiety to the Cross," in a painting by Tommaso Laureti on the ceiling of the Sala di Costantino (late sixteenth century).

IV. Blessed Michelina by Barocci (Vatican Pinacotheca); a representation that reflects the post-tridentine air of religious reassertion.

V. Pius VII placing Etruscan vases in the Library (fresco by Domenico de Angelis, c. 1818, in the Vatican Library); the pontificate of Pius VII marked the high point of the massive effort to safeguard the artistic patrimony of Rome, which was begun in the late eighteenth century.

II

III

IV

V

developed with exceptional vigor. Churches accumulated splendid furnishings and objects of sacred art, and high church dignitaries acquired incomparable treasures of classical, Renaissance and contemporary art.

In the eighteenth century, aesthetic doctrine found fertile ground in the dormant classicism of Roman culture. The popes—their aims were still apologetic—participated in the new fervor for classical studies and archaeological excavations, promoted the opening up to the public of their great artistic wealth and emanated previously unheard-of decrees to protect works of art.

The popularization of the Roman art collections, a process destined to endure for a century to come, commenced during the pontificate of Clement XII (1730-1740), when the great Capitoline collection was opened to the public for the first time.

The task of protecting the immense artistic wealth of Rome was taken up in a body of farsighted legislation, as the last act of a single, long-lived, uninterrupted cultural tradition extending from Classical to Christian Rome and from the age of Raphael to that of Winckelmann and Canova.

Pontifical collectors in our times have preferred to limit themselves to works of art explicitly referring to the mission of the church.

The Ethnological-Missionary Museum was established to "illustrate the labors of all those who seek to extend the reign of God on earth" (Pius XI), and the Collection of Modern Religious Art was founded by Pope Paul VI to document the capacity of contemporary art to express religious feeling.

Today the walls of the Vatican, solemn guardians of an inestimable artistic estate, have opened up to transmit to the world a message of hope and concord. From time to time, groups of art works selected in accord-

ance with strict standards have been sent abroad—seemingly an ideal escort of the reigning pontiff in his inexhaustible peregrinations across the globe—to bear witness to the beauty of God on earth and to the life of a universal, invincible cultural tradition.

122

122. Fresco with map of Italy (after a cartoon by Ignazio Danti, 1580-83), Gallery of Maps.

The Gallery of Maps

Gregory XIII, the pope who in 1582 promulgated the calendar reform and established the "Gregorian" calendar still in force today, was also responsible for the construction and decoration of the Gallery of Maps, a project which bears witness to his scientific interests. The gallery was built above Pirro Ligorio's west corridor and named for the forty map frescoes showing the topography of the regions of Italy and the possessions of the Church. The frescoes were painted between 1580 and 1583 after cartoons by the Dominican priest, Ignazio Dante, a distinguished geographer of the time and one of the chief authors of the Gregorian calendar reform. They are arranged along the walls with the space of the room to divide them as the Apennine Mountains divide Italy. On one wall are the regions bordering on the Ligurian and Tyrrhenian seas, on the other the regions bounded by the Alps and the Adriatic. At the northern end of the gallery is the Tower of the Winds, built especially for the astronomical observations required for the studies which preceded the promulgation of the new calendar.

123

124

The Vatican Library

The Vatican Library grew out of a manuscript collection of the early Renaissance that Pope Nicholas V kept in an as yet unidentified room of the papal palace. Nicholas V's intention to form a library was carried out by Sixtus IV, who established the first public library of Rome. It was located on the ground floor of the north wing of the palace and headed by the humanist historian and philosopher, Bartolomeo Platina. The collection of manuscripts—and later of printed volumes—continud to grow until at last the library rooms were insufficient to contain it. In 1587 Sixtus V ordered a new building which was built by Domenico Fontana across the middle of Bramante's Belvedere Courtyard. The Sistine Hall was named after the pope and is used as an exhibit room today. Originally it was the library reading room, and was decorated with frescoes illustrating episodes from the pontificate of Sixtus V, the great libraries of antiquity, the inventors of writing, and the councils of the Church. In the seventeenth century, new rooms were added by Paul V, Urban VIII, and Alexander VII along the gallery built by Pirro Ligorio. But the most important work was carried out during the eighteenth century. At this time a vast plan was undertaken to expand and reorganize the library collections. Clement XII created the gallery named after him—the Galleria Clementina—and enhanced the library with a collection of precious manuscripts, vases, and ancient medals.

123. Sistine Hall of the Vatican Library; the stories of the frescoes relate to the pontificate of Sixtus V.

124. Reliquary Cross of Paschal I (817-24), Museo Sacro, Vatican Library.

125

127

126

128

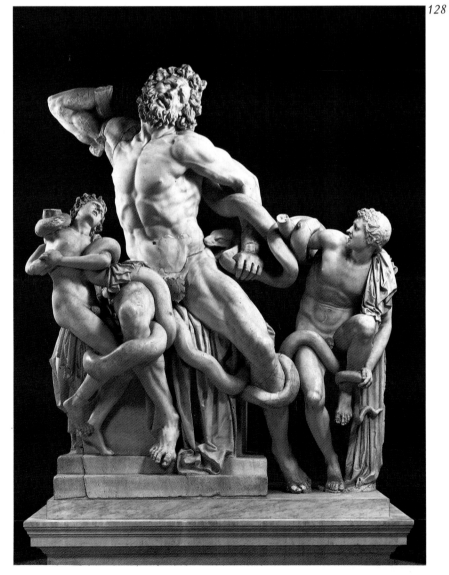

125. *Belvedere Apollo (Roman, A.D. 130-140, from a Greek bronze original of 330-320 B.C., probably by Leocares), Cortile Ottagono, Pio Clementine Museum.*

126. *Belvedere Torso (neo-Attic school of the first century B.C.), Sala delle Muse, Pio Clementine Museum.*

127. *Cortile ottagono, Pio Clementine Museum; this is the former Giardino degli Aranci, where Julius II kept his celebrated sculpture collection.*

129

130

Benedict XIV carried out one of his predecessor's projects in founding in 1756 a Museum of Christian Antiquities "to increase the splendor of Rome and to confirm religious truth through the evidence of Early Christian works." His Sacred Museum of the Vatican Library was the first "modern" museum of the Vatican. Later, in 1767, Clement XIII established the Profane Museum of the library, "to preserve the monuments of ancient Rome." Today, in addition to a rich group of illuminated manuscripts, the library contains collections of religious objects and furnishings (vestments, goldsmithery, enamels, and glass) that provide a documentary history of the minor arts from medieval to modern times, as well as many examples of Etruscan, Roman and Early Christian art.

131

The Museums

The collections of the Pio-Clementine Museum, like the Vatican Library collections, date back to the Renaissance. More specifically, they originated with the group of classical statues that Julius II placed in the courtyard of the Palazzetto del Belvedere. The *Apollo*, *Laocoön*, and Julius' other statues were the hub around which the Vatican collection of ancient art developed over the centuries. Julius's successors added new works to his collection, and the pontificates of Julius III and Marcellus II were graced with the first collection of "objects of art" to belong to the library. Pius V, inspired by the spirit of the Counterreformation, "censured"the classical collections and removed many of the works from the Vatican. For many years his successors were completely indifferent to collecting. How-

128. Laocoön (Rhodes, first century B.C. – first century A.D.), Cortile Ottagono, Pio Clementine Museum.

129. Sala Rotonda, Pio Clementine Museum.

130. The Muse Thalia (Roman sculpture based on a Greek original), Sala delle Muse, Pio Clementine Museum.

131. Julius Caesar (imperial Roman sculpture), Sala dei Busti, Pio Clementine Museum.

132

134

133

132. *Augustus of Prima Porta (A.D.
14-29), Braccio Nuovo; a remarkable example of Augustan classicism, found near
Livia's celebrated villa at Prima Porta.*

133. *Child Holding a Goose (Roman copy
of a Greek original of 300 B.C., attributed
to Boethos), Galleria dei Candelabri.*

134. *Galleria Lapidaria; the epigraphic
collection includes inscriptions sacred (on the
right) and profane (left).*

ever a renewed interest in ancient art that grew up in Rome at the
beginning of the eighteenth century led to several extraordinary ex-
hibitions.

In 1771, Clement XIV began the construction of what was then
one of the largest museums in the world, the Pio-Clementine Museum, completed by his successor Pius VI. To provide the museum
with a suitable location, a new building connecting the library with
the Palazzetto del Belvedere was erected and several rooms of the
older wings were either renovated or transformed. The courtyard in
which Julius II's *Apollo* and *Laocoön* were displayed was enclosed by
an octagonal portico. The loggia of the Palazzetto del Belvedere was
closed to create a new Gallery of Statues. In this typical example of
eighteenth-century museum organization, the works of art were
placed in their architectural settings as decorative pieces. Among the
rooms of the new building were the Sala Rotonda, modelled after
the Pantheon; the Room of the Muses and Room of the Animals,
which received their names from the works on display; and the Cabinet of the Masks, named for the subject of the floor mosaic taken
from Hadrian's Villa. Despite the fact that these new rooms had
been built specifically for the works of art they held, there too art
was treated as ornament. Although the criteria used in organizing
the displays is outdated today, the Pio-Clementine Museum was
planned as an organic whole, based on valid archaeological informa-
tion. It represented the first step to a scientific approach to the world
of classical antiquity and the first example of a rational attitude toward museum management.

In 1785, the Gallery of the Candelabra was designed by the architects who had completed the new wings of the Pio-Clementine
Museum, Michelangelo Simonetti and Giuseppe Camporese.

Pius VII, elected to the papacy in 1800, was responsible for the
establishment of the Chiaramonti Museum—Chiaramonti was the
pontiff's surname—and the definitive organization of the epigraphi-
cal collection begun by Clement XIV in the Galleria Lapidaria, Bra-

135

136

137

138

135. Imperial Roman busts in the Chiaramonti Museum; the gallery retains the original layout by Antonio Canova.

136. Minerva and Marsias (Roman copy of a fifth century B.C. Greek original in bronze possibly by Myron), Gregorian Profane Museum.

137. Funerary stele with young athlete (Greece, fifth century B.C.), Sala degli Originali Greci; one of the precious Greek originals in the Vatican.

138. The Good Shepherd (Early Christian, third century A.D.), Pio Christian Museum; a representation of Christ still showing a late-classical taste.

139

141

140

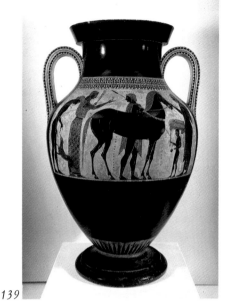

139. Black-figure amphora with the Departure of the Dioscuri (Athens, c. 540 B.C., signed by Exechias) Gregorian Etruscan Museum.

140. Mars of Todi (Italic sculpture, c. 400 B.C.), Gregorian Etruscan Museum; a cult statue representing a warrior, found in 1835 at Todi.

141. The Vatican Museums as seen from the dome of St. Peter's with the Cortile della Pigna and, in the foreground, the transversal galleries of the Vatican Library and the Braccio Nuovo.

mante's long corridor connecting the papal palace with the Palazzetto del Belvedere. He was also responsible for the construction of a new wing of the museums, the "Braccio Nuovo" which further divided Bramante's courtyard, facing the monumental Nicchione della Pigna (built by Pirro Ligorio in about 1565) on one side and the Vatican Library on the other. Thus, two new courtyards were created—the Cortile della Pigna and the Library Courtyard.

The galleries of the nineteenth-century Braccio Nuovo, which were filled with Greek and Roman sculpture, represented a significant step in the direction of modern museology. The architectural setting was now organized exclusively for the preservation and display of the works of art. By the time that they were completed, the eighteenth-century revival of archaeological studies, the success of neoclassicism, and Winckelmann's contributions to classical criticism were past history. Antonio Canova was the present Superintendent of the Fine Arts in Rome, and the Vatican collections had become an organic group of works based on a sound knowledge of archaeology and developing along lines established in a well-thought-out museum acquisition and display program.

In 1837, Gregory XVI inaugurated the Etruscan Museum, and two years later, the Egyptian Museum. Thus, the Vatican collections, until that time mainly composed of Greek and Roman art, were extended to other civilizations. The Etruscan collection consists of objects found during the fervid excavations that were undertaken in the years when Etruscan studies was a newborn discipline. The Regolini Galassi Tomb, with its rich furnishings, was uncovered in 1836-37; the bronze called the *Mars of Todi* was found in 1935; pottery and clay objects in great abundance were retrieved from Cerveteri; and innumerable specimens of imported Greek ceramics were discovered, especially at Vulci.

The Egyptian collection contained objects and works of art that came from monuments and ancient collections located mainly in the area of Rome and its environs. Despite the fanciful decorative setting, it was organized with the intent to launch a new, scientific methodology in the study of ancient Egyptian art and culture. Re-

142

143

144

145

142. *The Sala Regolini Galassi in the Gregorian Etruscan Museum with the impressive collection of the Sorbo Necropolis at Cerveteri.*

143. *Relief of the deceased at table (Egypt, Eighth Dynasty, c. 1350 B.C.), Gregorian Egyptian Museum.*

144. *Statue of Amun Ra (Egypt, Nineteenth Dynasty, Reign of Sety I (Before 1000 B.C.), Gregorian Egyptian Museum.*

145. *Gildes wood Death Mask (Egypt, 323-30 B.C.), Gregorian Egyptian Museum.*

History of the Papal States
by *Giancarlo Mori*

In canonic doctrine, the legal basis for temporal sovereignty has always been encapsulated in the principal of guaranteed, absolute independence for the pope for the exercise of his spiritual power. This principle was realized in history slowly and gradually, in the course of a process which transformed a once exiguous territory into a full-fledged state. For over ten centuries, with various ups and downs, the pope has thus ruled his own state—the Papal States—as an absolute sovereign, running foreign policy, collecting taxes from his subjects, minting coins, and making laws at all levels.

At first the pope was simply a subject of the Roman Empire. But, from the fourth century on, he enjoyed special honors, and with the advent of Justinian (554) he acquired jurisdiction over certain civil and financial cases. Pelagius I (555-561) made use of these powers in the preliminary organization of a number of territories given to the church by endowment—the so-called "Patrimony of St. Peter."

In 726, the Duchy of Rome came under papal jurisdiction, and Spoleto and the Marca Picena spontaneously submitted to it in 729, but it was with the Carolingian emperors that the Papal States—then far-flung domains—first acquired real stability. When the fortune of the Carolingian dynasty came to an end, the Papal States again lay at the mercy of the Roman nobility, and by 1000 they had practically become a feud of the Germanic empire.

From that time on, the recovery of autonomy and temporal power for the popes progressed at the same rate as their disengagement from imperial interference in spiritual matters. But the process was not smooth and continuous. On the contrary, it was absolutely unpredictable, full of enormous changes, ups and downs, sudden and unexpected breaks, and it made instability one of the major characteristics of the history of the papacy. Thus, on the one hand, as early as the eleventh century, the papal territory was structured in provinces: Benevento, Campania, Spoleto, the Patrimony of St. Peter and the other Umbrian dioceses, Ancona and Urbino, Romagna, Bologna. On the other hand, the relative sovereignty of these provinces was increasingly compromised by a diffused state of anarchy. In Rome itself, the intrigues of the nobility were bound up with popular uprisings. The Manfredi, Malatesta and Ordelaffi families rent the Marches and Romagna. Bologna was sold by the Pepoli to the Duchy of Milan. And things were no better outside the Papal States, for the events connected with the Avignon period (1309-77) and the Western schism (1378-1417) favored the rise of theories that ran contrary to the very principle of legitimacy of the Papal States.

An early attempt at military and political recovery began with Cardinal Albornoz (1300-67). He toppled the Roman Republic of Cola di Rienzo (1352), and regained the Marches and a good part of Romagna and Bologna.

Later, Cardinal Bellarmino (1542-1621), the great theoretician of the Catholic Reformation, undertook to demonstrate that the juridical validity of temporal power derives from the nature of the primacy itself. Since by nature the primacy requires absolute autonomy, by divine right it must

The Roman-Byzantine dominions in the age of Justinian (left).
The Papal States around the mid nineteenth century (right): territories annexed to the Kingdom of Italy in 1860 (light brown), and to Italy in October 1870 (dark brown).

enjoy immunity within all national and international political orders. Such immunity can be acquired only through real temporal sovereignty.

In a way, the fifteenth and sixteenth centuries represented the apex of this sovereignty. The popes were virtual princes involved in all the major political events of the time. They were skillful diplomats and refined patrons of the arts.

But by sanctioning the secularization of the church's possessions, the Peace of Westphalia (1648) did away with the political organization of Christianity, and weakened the image and the power of the pope-king. The negative consequences of the sale of a wide range of administrative powers by an increasingly isolated papal government in dire economic straits increased during the following century. Individual jurisdictions thus were wedded more and more to the privileges of the nobility.

It took the painful experience with Napoleon to suggest the first real reform of the papal government (1816). Inspired by Cardinal Consalvi and based on the principles of centralization, uniformity, and separation of the civil and ecclesiastical governments, it eliminated the extreme intricacies of local legislation, defined and limited the various spheres of power.

But the resistance of the ecclesiastical ruling class forced Leo XII (1824) to deny the spirit of Consalvi's reform, and the abuse of administrative and judicial powers was added to the uncertainties of the law. Thus as early as 1830, especially in Romagna and the Marches, the liberal movement found increasing support among the discontented populace, previously won over to the order of the Napoleonic system. Gregory XVI offered a few judical reforms (1831-1834), and Pius IX the amnesty of 1848 followed by the Constitution, in an unsuccessful endeavor to prop up the already tottering Church rule.

The annexation of the Marches and Umbria to the Kingdom of Sardinia (1860)

forced Pius IX into a position of absolute intransigence. He excommunicated the "usurpers" and in his Syllabus of 1864 condemned the thesis according to which "the abolition of the temporal power would lead to the freedom and happiness of the Church." He refused even to take into consideration what had become an inescapable reality— Italy, in the hands of the liberals, was already on the way to becoming a unified constitutional state.

When the Papal States, reduced by then to just Rome and its environs, were abandoned by Austria as well, the train of events rapidly moved on to the conclusion of September 20, 1870, and the "Roman Question" entered its crucial phase. The "Law of Guarantees" of 1871 was meant to secure the prerogatives necessary to the pope in the exercise of his spiritual power. But Pius IX declared the guarantees illusory and insufficient, refused the indemnity that accompanied them and retired into a self-imposed retreat in his palaces at the Vatican.

The reconciliation between the two banks of the Tiber began in 1904 with the partial abolition of the ruling that prohibited Catholics from taking part in political life. But it did not become definitive until the advent of the fascist regime. It was then that the Lateran Treaty (1929) was signed by the Italian State and the Holy See. The Lateran Treaty definitively closed the Roman Question. The Holy See recognized the annexations of 1870 and the territorial integrity of the Kingdom of Italy, and the Italian government provided the guarantees necessary to the exercise "in absolute and visible independence" of an "incontestable sovereignty" inherent in the very nature of the Holy See.

Successive international procedure showed the unique system set up by the Lateran Treaty to be a valid means of safeguarding the pope's spiritual power. The Catholic Church is the hierarchically organized supranational community of all baptized people wherever they reside. The Holy See is

the governmental body, with an international legal personality, through which the pope exercises the sovereign authority indispensible to the free exercise of spiritual power connected with the primacy. Therefore, it is also the body that protects the interests of the Catholic Church and the individual national Churches in the international community.

I. The "Patrimony of St. Peter," first core of the Papal States, toward the end of the sixteenth century in a fresco by Ignazio Danti (Gallery of Maps).

II. Maps of the papal States.

III. Clement VII meeting with Francis I: the diplomatic rapprochement with the French monarchy to the detriment of Charles V led to the sack of Rome in 1527 (painting by Giorgio Vasari and assistants, Florence, Palazzo Vecchio).

IV. Urban VIII building Forte Urbano (tapestry from the Barberini workshops; Vatican, Galleria degli Arazzi). Urban VIII succeeded in annexing the Duchy of Urbino to the Papal States, in 1631, and he intervened in numerous other political questions.

V. Pius IX blessing the allied armies at Gaeta in may 1849 (print by Senen Buenga; Rome, Museo del Risorgimento).

VI. Italian troops enter Rome on 20 September 1870 through a breach in the walls near Porta Pia (Carlo Ademollo, Milan, Museo del Risorgimento).

146

147

146. Giotto, Stefaneschi Triptych, the back without the predella (c. 1315), Pinacoteca; executed for the high altar of Old St. Peter's.

147. Melozzo da Forlì, Sixtus IV and the Platina (1477), Pinacoteca.

148. Raphael, Crowning of the Virgin (1502-03), Pinacoteca; one of the artist's first works.

149. Raphael, Transfiguration (1517-20), Pinacoteca; one of the artist's more outstanding achievements, painted shortly before his death.

150. La Pesca Miracolosa (tapestry woven by Pieter van Aelst after a design by Raphael, c. 1515), Pinacoteca.

151. Leonardo da Vinci, St. Jerome (c. 1480), Pinacoteca.

148

149

150

151

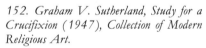

152. Graham V. Sutherland, Study for a Crucifixion (1947), Collection of Modern Religious Art.

153. Emile Nolde, Priest (1939-45), Collection of Modern Religious Art.

154. Odilon Redon, Joan of Arc (late nineteenth – early twentieth century), Collection of Modern Religious Art.

cently it was reordered, but parts of the old, now outdated decor were preserved as a record of the exhibit criteria of nineteenth century museology, which sought—albeit naively—to recreate what was believed to be the original setting and atmosphere of the works.

The present century has seen the establishment of the Vatican Pinacoteca, dedicated to paintings and tapestries illustrating the history of European painting from the eleventh to the nineteenth century. Located in a building inaugurated by Pius XI in 1932, the new Pinacoteca brought to a happy conclusion the complicated history of an unsettled collection, founded by Pius VI 150 years earlier, enriched by his successor, but devoid of a definitive location and organization.

Pope John XXIII created two new museums, the Gregorian Profane and the Pio Christian museum, housed in a special structure erected in accordance with the most up-to-date standards of architecture and museology and containing the collections of Greco-Roman sculpture and Early Christian objects previously kept in the palace of the Lateran.

Pope John XXIII also transferred from the Lateran the Ethnological Missionary Museum, founded by Pius XI "to illustrate the labors of all those who seek to extend the reign of God on earth." This museum displays objects produced by extra-European cultures. They come from Catholic missions throughout the world.

155

The most recent museums are the Historical Museum (1973), established by Paul VI to exhibit the relics of the ancient papal States, and the Collection of Modern Religious Art, also founded by Pope Paul VI. Located in the Borgia Apartments and the rooms below the Sistine Chapel, it was incorporated into the great iconographical tradition of the papacy to provide a record of the work of modern artists who attempt to represent subjects connected with the teachings of the Church.

155. Armor of a knight of the personal guard of Pius VI (late eighteenth century), Historic Museum.

156. Horse (China, Tang Dynasty, seventh–tenth century A.D.), Ethnological Missionary Museum.

157. African Mask, Ethnological Missionary Museum.

History of the Papacy
by Giancarlo Mori

In the year 64 (or 67) of the Common Era, Peter the Apostle died a victim of Nero's persecutions and was buried near the site of his martyrdom on the Vatican Hill. Recent archaeological findings (1976) seem to prove the fact. But there is a far more ancient proof in the evidence of the cult worship practiced in that place, for it had become sacred for numerous pilgrims.

The basilica resolved upon by Constantine and completely rebuilt between the sixteenth and seventeenth centuries symbolizes the connection between that evidence and the faith that it produced. By virtue of that faith, the apostolic primacy of Peter was wedded to the place of his martyrdom and eventually became the primacy of the bishop of Rome. Its permanent structure was the papacy.

Thus, the third successor of Peter, the Roman bishop St. Clement (88-97), could demand complete obedience of the Christians of Corinth, and Pope Victor (189-199) could excommunicate several Eastern bishops by invoking the authority of Peter and Paul. The procedure first took the form of doctrine with Pope St. Zosimus (417-418), but the events and his actions made Leo I (440-461) the first real "pope." He intervened with the bishops of Gaul, proclaimed the Council of Chalcedon and regained papal authority over the patriarch of Alexandria.

Once the primacy was well-consolidated within the church, a clash with royal power became inevitable. St. Gelasius I (492-496) had already invoked the papal authority's right of control over the exercise of royal power, a theory which was carried to its extremes in the bull Unam Sanctam of Boniface VIII (1295-1303). It proclaimed that both spiritual and temporal power are founded on Church authority, the former being exercised directly by the Church in the person of the priest, and the latter being exercised by the king for the Church, subject to the will of the pope.

Thus the premises were laid for the enervating conflict between Church and State, especially because two events of truly great significance had taken place in the meantime. Leo XIII (795-816) had enthroned Charlemagne and proclaimed him "Augustus, crowned by God," thereby creating an initial division between the Roman and Byzantine churches, subjecting himself in point of fact to the imperial authority and laying the foundations for an enduring Christian empire. St. Gregory VII (1073-1085) had wanted to win back for the church alone the right to confer ecclesiastical offices and had vigorously fought Henry IV with his deposi-

tions and excommunications. In the twenty-seven propositions of the so-called Dictatus Papae he claimed the supreme authority of the pontiff over the church and the state.

But even in those early times the pope also exercised his primacy in the specific sphere of ecclesiastical organization and discipline. With St. Gregory I (590-604), there had been the reform of the liturgy, the Gregorian Chant, and the spread of the Benedictine rule; with St. Nicholas I (858-867), the reorganization of the Frankish Church, sacramental discipline and papal intervention when the imperial chancellor Photius was illegally elected Patriarch of Contantinople; with Innocent III (1198-1216), the first mendicant orders, the centralization of the Holy See and the Albigensian Crusade; with Gregory IX (1227-1241), the first attempt at the codification of canon law.

In short, the papacy was growing into a solid structure. It was solid enough to withstand the abuses of a generally corrupt clergy and the consequent challenge of vast reform movements that shook the Church to its very foundations. Rather than prevailing, these

REXROGAT ABBATEM: MATHILDIM SUPPLICAT ATR; 5

I

factors set in motion a magnificent, centralized, Roman Catholic offensive.

It was Paul III's (1534-1549) merit to have overcome his predecessors' hesitations and convened a council (at Trent) for the reform of the Church. But only with Pius IV (1560-1565) were decrees emanated on the sources of Revelation, original sin, the nature of the sacraments, diocesan synods, and pastoral visits. St. Pius V (1566-1572) proceeded with the reform of the clergy, the residence of the bishops and the religious orders, and promulgated the Roman Catechism, the Breviary and the Missal. And Gregory XIII (1572-1585), in order to have better control of the application of the Tridentine decrees, substituted for the papal legates permanent, accredited representatives to civil government: the Nuncios who were later to play such an important role in the relationship between single Churches and their nation-states.

In the two centuries preceding the French Revolution, not a single pope was capable of grasping the complicated problems involved in the slow evolution of a secular, constitutional state or of understanding the complex relationship between faith and reason. This long period of incomprehension led to the reappraisal, inside and outside the Church, of the primacy of the pope. The episode involving the Pistoiese bishop Scipione de' Ricci contained a warning of what was to come. A diocesan synod that he convened deliberated a number of proposals concerning doctrine and discipline, and Pius VI (1775-1799) declared eighty-five of them to be erroneous. Among other things, the erroneous proposals had to do with the authority of the Church, the natural and supernatural condition of man, and the sacraments.

But far, far weightier consequences came of the concordat with Napoleon (1801), signed by Pius VII (1800-1823); for it brought about the increasing constriction of the Holy

II

See in the exercise of its primatial functions.

At last, the whole of the nineteenth century was virtually dominated by the mainly ideological conflict between the Church and the world. The Syllabus of Pius IX (1846-1878) against rationalism, liberalism, socialism, communism, and freethinking was just the first oppressive chapter of the story. It was later complemented by Pius X's (1903-1914) encyclical Pascendi regarding the "modernist" errors in philosophical, dogmatic, and apologetic principles and the principles of historical criticism. The dogmatic enunciation of the primacy of the Roman pontiff and the infallibility of the papal office also emanated by Pius IX, represents an extreme ideological reaction to the clearly definitive expropriation of an age-old exercise of power.

But preoccupations of a different sort were also slowly ripening. Leo XIII (1878-1903), with the encyclical Rerum Novarum, laid the foundations for a modern Christian doctrine of work. Benedict XV (1914-1922), with the promulgation of the first Code of Canon Law, effectively granted recognition to the principles of clarity and equity, which had been invoked by many for Church law. And Pius XI (1922-1939) at last healed the terrible wounds opened in 1870 with the "Roman Question" by signing the Lateran Treaty and Concordat (1929) with the Italian State.

The Holy See was slowly reorganizing, and the new order was to be entirely different from the one known to the past. A strong, moderately enlightened papacy was needed, a papacy with a reassuring style in managing the spheres of doctrine and theology. The intense pontificate of Pius XII (1939-1958) fitted these requirements to a tee. Pastoral liturgy, Bible studies, missionary and ecumenical problems—they all received new consideration under the pope, but not without painful incidents. Among the latter were the events connected with the political climate of the period—the Mindszenty, Slipyi and Wyszynski cases, the cases of the "Church of Silence."

But new hopes were ripening, hopes for which the brief, but intense pontificate of John XXIII (1958-1963) opened horizons absolutely unthinkable only a few years before him. Pope John was probably the first pope in the history of the Church to convene an ecumenical council not to "affirm" but simply to discuss. The dialogue was opened to all—believers and non-believers, insiders and outsiders, the Churches of the East and the West. The contemporaneous decision to revise the Code of Canon Law of 1917 revealed the profound humility of a pontificate that meant to read "the signs of the times" by calling itself into question first.

Paul VI (1963-1978) brought to these new activities an attitude of pastoral sollicitude open to the contradictions and uncertainties of his time. To his credit there occurred, among other things, the internationalization of the Curia Romana, the introduction of laymen into the church at various levels, the first albeit timid steps on the road to effective episcopal collegiality, and the diplomatic opening to the countries of Eastern Europe.

October 1978 ushered in Pope John Paul I's few weeks of rule, now more the subject of anecdote than of history. Then came the great innovation—the first non-Italian pope in four centuries. John Paul II (December 1978) is trying to coagulate tensions and hopes, dissension and consensus, and is using great ductility to invent a new role—the role of the leader—for the Apostolic See.

I. The fight for investiture: Henry IV implores Mathilde of Canossa to intercede on his behalf with Gregory VII (original chronicle of the life of Mathilde of Canossa, eleventh century).

II. The Council of Trent in a painting of the sixteenth-century Venetian school (Paris, Louvre).

III. The incoronation ceremony of Napoleon I in the church of Notre Dame in the presence of Pius VII (detail of the painting by Jacques-Louis David, Paris, Louvre).

IV. John XXIII receiving the bishops opening day of the Second Vatican Council (11 October 1962) in a relief on the Porta della Morte by Giacomo Manzù.

List of Popes Mentioned

List of Artists Mentioned

Distributed in Rome by A.T.S. ITALIA, Via F. Sivori, 6
tel. 06/39726079, fax 06/39726080